SIMPLIFY
YOUR
LIFE

SIMPLIFY
YOUR
LIFE

WASTE LESS
VALUE MORE
GO MINIMALIST

MARY CONROY

HAY HOUSE

Carlsbad, California • New York City
London • Sydney • New Delhi

Published in the United Kingdom by:
Hay House UK Ltd, The Sixth Floor, Watson House,
54 Baker Street, London W1U 7BU
Tel: +44 (0)20 3927 7290; Fax: +44 (0)20 3927 7291
www.hayhouse.co.uk

Published in the United States of America by:
Hay House Inc., PO Box 5100, Carlsbad, CA 92018-5100
Tel: (1) 760 431 7695 or (800) 654 5126
Fax: (1) 760 431 6948 or (800) 650 5115; www.hayhouse.com

Published in Australia by:
Hay House Australia Pty Ltd, 18/36 Ralph St, Alexandria NSW 2015
Tel: (61) 2 9669 4299; Fax: (61) 2 9669 4144; www.hayhouse.com.au

Published in India by:
Hay House Publishers India, Muskaan Complex,
Plot No.3, B-2, Vasant Kunj, New Delhi 110 070
Tel: (91) 11 4176 1620; Fax: (91) 11 4176 1630; www.hayhouse.co.in

The information given in this book should not be treated as a substitute
for professional medical advice; always consult a medical practitioner. Any
use of information in this book is at the reader's discretion and risk. Neither
the author nor the publisher can be held responsible for any loss, claim or
damage arising out of the use, or misuse, of the suggestions made, the
failure to take medical advice or for any material on third-party websites.

Names and identifying details have been changed to protect the privacy of
individuals.

A catalogue record for this book is available from the British Library.

Tradepaper ISBN: 978-1-78817-444-2
E-book ISBN: 978-1-78817-445-9
Audiobook ISBN: 978-1-78817-456-5

MIX
Paper from
responsible sources
FSC
www.fsc.org   FSC® C013056

Printed and bound in Great Britain by
TJ International Ltd, Padstow, Cornwall

CONTENTS

INTRODUCTION

When most people think of minimalism, their minds usually conjure up an image of sixties-style design, of expensive Scandinavian-style furniture placed sparingly in large, loft-style apartments. There's probably a young couple in a pared-down designer kitchen, relaxing at the end of the day with a bottle of wine they've opened with a Philippe Starck corkscrew, both of them dressed in simple but stylish monochrome clothing.

It all seems rather joyless, doesn't it?

Especially when you consider that the essence of minimalism, as a way of life that's being adopted by more and more people in the 21st century, is the pursuit of our true passions by jettisoning things – both material and intangible – that are simply not serving us.

In the years immediately after the global financial crash of 2008, there was a vogue for newspaper articles and TV programs about individuals who had divested themselves of their worldly goods and embraced a new life away from the excesses of their old lifestyles. The reports often focused on the contrast between their previous lives as, say, high-octane executives, and their new, humbler circumstances, but failed to address the psychological journey these individuals had taken. Invariably, the former financier or stock trader would be quoted as saying that they didn't miss their old company car or executive credit card, and that life was better now, with fewer material possessions and more time to spend with friends and family.

I'd argue that these articles and TV features only told half the story. They showed that the process of ridding yourself of many of the trappings of so-called success could be incredibly liberating. But they left readers and viewers with the impression that, realistically, only a person on a six-figure salary has the means to implement such changes in their life.

Minimalism is really about understanding
what it means to have a meaningful life, one
that's defined by our individual values.

The philosophy is a simple one, and it can be extended to many areas of our lives – our homes, personal belongings, work, finances, relationships, our lives online, even our health.

As we enter a new decade, the advocates for minimalism tend to be young people who look good in a black T-shirt and have a winning way with a TED Talk audience. But minimalism is a concept that can be adopted by anybody, at any stage of their lives. It can help the college undergraduate who is starting to forge the values that will take him through a career, the young mother who is trying to keep her family's household clutter under control, and even the recently retired, who are surveying their new lives.

With its focus on conscious consumption as opposed to unthinking compulsive purchasing, minimalism also provides people with the psychological breathing space to consider how their retail choices are affecting the environment and themselves.

The aim of minimalism isn't to part us from our most cherished possessions, to have us living in a bare, impersonal room with just a chair, table, and bed to call our own.

More than a design aesthetic, minimalism is a way of life that allows us to strip away the clutter that gets in the way of us achieving our goals. It allows us to clarify our thinking and reduce the mental chatter so that we can gain insight into ourselves and set a course for the life that we really want for ourselves.

GOOD HABITS FOR A GOOD LIFE

At its core, minimalism is about re-establishing what is of value in your life and letting go of everything that's not. It means focusing on what's important and recognizing what is nothing more than distraction. It means learning to listen to your own needs and investing in the greatest asset you'll ever own: yourself.

Before we look at how you can improve your life, let's look at how you got to where you are today.

First of all, where are you? Right now. Have you just grabbed five minutes to sit down at the kitchen table with a cup of coffee? If that's the case, it stands to reason that you're living in a warm, dry home where you're sufficiently on top of things to pay the gas and electricity bills. That's a considerable achievement. The coffee pot may sit just a few inches away from your kitchen's clutter drawer, with its mangled, chaotic mess of old cell chargers, miscellaneous bakeware and correspondence waiting to be filed, but the fact that you're able to make a cup of coffee and sit down at a kitchen table in a warm home represents the culmination of good choices you've made over the years

Or perhaps you're sitting on a bus on the morning commute to work (possibly fantasizing about being able to while away a few minutes at the kitchen table instead of being jostled by fellow commuters). Then you also deserve to be congratulated. You may feel like a drone, completing unchallenging tasks for a thankless boss; you may even suspect that your late-night online shopping sprees are a reaction to feeling powerless in your life. But you made it to the bus stop this morning; you were organized enough to find a smart outfit to wear, to have your phone charged up, and find your bus fare. That all points to a person who is self-reliant and has developed a repertoire of habits (or hacks) to ease their way past most of life's speed bumps.

Wherever you are, whatever you're doing, no matter how unglamorous or uninspiring your life may appear to you, if you're able to feed yourself, clothe yourself, pay the rent or mortgage, you're already a winner. You're already reaping the rewards of habits you've honed over the decades. The good news is that minimalism is merely the development of new habits – habits that will move you closer toward the life you truly want to live.

EXPLODING THE MYTHS

First, let's clear up some of the myths about minimalism. Like all myths, some of them contain an element of truth, but they also contain fears we harbor about our own lives and where we might be failing.

MYTH 1: YOUR HOUSE WILL BECOME AN EMPTY, IMPERSONAL SHELL

When people hear the word 'minimalism,' they often associate it with homes that have open living spaces, rather than family rooms, and walls stripped bare of art, mementos, even family photographs; with kitchens that are master classes in design rather than serving as the heart of a family home. While it's true that minimalists are in favor of removing extraneous clutter, it's not fair to say that their homes end up becoming impersonal, cold, bare shells.

> Look around you. How many of the items
> you see actually bring value to your life?

The novelty coasters, the pullout cookery supplement that came free with a newspaper six months ago but still hasn't migrated to your kitchen, the pile of CDs you haven't played in five years: What value do they bring to your life? Now imagine that all of the items that bring little value to your life are magically removed from view. What's left? The love seat you bought when you moved in with your partner. Your collection of family photographs. The table that your family gathers around every evening.

In this thought exercise, what have you lost? Nothing more than rather worthless junk that brings nothing to your life. What remains are the possessions that have value and add meaning to your life.

MYTH 2: YOU MIGHT BE VIEWED AS A CHEAPSKATE

Many of us have grown up in a culture where success isn't only celebrated, it's literally worn on our sleeves. And driven on the road. And showcased in our homes. So when minimalists try to unhitch 'success' from the material goods that are supposed to symbolize it, it can be unsettling for people who aren't minimalists. 'All the money she must be on – and she won't even buy herself a new smartphone!' I heard somebody mutter one day about a mutual acquaintance. Firstly, it says much about the empty inner life of any person who has the time to speculate on the way anybody else conducts their lives. But also, minimalists simply make different choices about how they spend their money. Ultimately, how you choose to spend your money is your business, but if a minimalist manages to make financial savings by leading a pared-down lifestyle, they'll often instead spend their money on personal projects, travel, helping family out, or boosting their contributions to charity. Practitioners of minimalism know that success can be celebrated in many different ways.

MYTH 3: A MINIMALIST LIFE IS LONELY AND BORING

The popular image of the typical minimalist home bears a striking resemblance to the home decor of a particularly ascetic monk. Many people think that, by trying not to accrue possessions, minimalists sit at a bare table at dinner time, setting a place for themselves with their lone dinner plate and the sole mug in their crockery collection.

That's far too dreary for me! I much prefer my own kitchen table, with its mismatched mugs, pasta bowls, and side plates, and where the centerpiece is a small vase filled with flowers or even simple greenery.

There can also be a general feeling that the minimalist lifestyle is so extreme that it creates barriers between the people who practice it and their friends. In fact, most people who follow a minimalist lifestyle find that their lives actually open up. They find they have more time for fun activities with the children instead of devoting hours of the weekend to housework. They can make plans to visit friends because they're not caught up in consuming social media. Or they can go traveling because they have a bit more spare cash.

Spending quality time with our children, creating wonderful memories with our friends, seeing the world – none of those activities would qualify as 'boring' for most people I know.

MYTH 4: YOU'LL NEVER OWN NICE THINGS

Minimalists aim to break the cycle of perpetually shopping and mindlessly buying consumer goods ad nauseam. This doesn't stop them having a keen eye for an antique armchair made by a master craftsman, or a powerful camera that will help them in their business. Minimalists can't avoid buying goods in today's world. But they try to make conscious choices about consumption. Instead of buying five cheap sweaters in five different colors, the minimalist will opt for a good-quality brand where the manufacturer uses ethically sourced raw ingredients and pays the workers a decent living wage. Then they'll buy one sweater.

Ultimately, minimalism is about becoming
aware of your power as a consumer,
and thinking more deeply about how
you use your disposable income.

Meanwhile, minimalism also encourages people to live within their means, eschewing the manner in which shopping has become a pastime and something that permits people to build up potentially devastating credit card debt. Our first financial responsibility is to ourselves, and getting into debt over consumer spending serves absolutely nobody. But marshaling our resources through innately frugal minimalism can help us to acquire those 'nice things' without being left with a legacy of debt.

MYTH 5: MINIMALISM IS TOO HARD CORE

Minimalism has been 'having a moment' in recent times. In the years immediately after the Great Recession of 2008, minimalism's principles of reining in spending and reducing conspicuous consumption chimed with a generation that had experienced firsthand the uncertainty of rampant capitalism and the aftereffects of calamitous lending policies. Saddled with student debt and uncertain whether they would ever be able to afford to buy their own home, young people found themselves looking at alternatives to the spend-spend-spend, consume-consume-consume culture in which their parents had indulged.

Part of that pushback in recent years has been the wider adoption of veganism and the increased profile of environmental concerns and zero-waste objectives. It's true that some minimalists came to the lifestyle because minimalism complements veganism, environmentalism, and zero-waste concerns. But minimalism has lots to offer everybody, whether you're a young, single person starting out in life, a senior trying to declutter, or even a family caught up in the hustle and bustle of juggling school runs with playdates.

MYTH 6: MINIMALISM IS UNFAIR ON CHILDREN

In many ways, this myth cuts to the heart of why minimalism is in need of an image makeover. For many people who don't engage in the lifestyle, minimalism appears to leave little room for personality or individuality, and even less for the random yet joy-filled chaos of family life. Critics of minimalism harbor fear that children growing up in homes where minimalism is practiced are denied their right to a coterie of their own toys and, more heartbreakingly, will be frozen out of friendships with children who are more plugged-in to pop culture.

Nobody – not even the strictest minimalist – would deny their children their most cherished toys in the interest of maintaining some sort of lifestyle idyll. But adults vastly overestimate how many toys children actually play with, and while the parents of young children may believe that their home will be forever awash with flimsy plastic toys, it's a phase that eventually passes.

Sometimes those who criticize minimalism within families are guilty of projecting an outdated idyll of childhood onto the next generation, of perpetually trying to recreate the scenes of abundance that characterized Western society from the 1980s onward. But parents who practice minimalism are often following in their own parents' and grandparents' footsteps, instilling in their children the values of thrift and resourcefulness that helped earlier generations survive and thrive. Meanwhile, many parents have seen the effect that plastics have on the environment or feel uneasy about consumer culture gaining a foothold in their families. For them, minimalism offers a way through the almost endemic forces urging us to endlessly consume.

MYTH 7: MINIMALISM IS ABOUT TURNING BACK THE CLOCK

It's true that minimalists like to work toward the point where they can shed many of the accouterments of modern life. Many people in the minimalist movement try to live within their means, to remove much of the clutter from their homes, and live their lives in a simpler mode. But that's not to say that they're rejecting the 21st century. Minimalists are likely to be more judicious users of technology than their contemporaries, but that doesn't mean they want to turn back time.

People who practice minimalism are fully cognizant of the values of modern technology. However, very often they've decided that they'll no longer be slaves to social media or any other form of technology that's chipping away at their personal time. Minimalism isn't about turning back the clock; it's about evolving to a point where technology is a tool that we use, not something to which we slavishly give over our precious time.

MYTH 8: THERE'S NO ROOM FOR SENTIMENT

This is a powerful argument against minimalism. For many people, minimalism conjures an image of family heirlooms being cast into a dumpster on a whim, or a carefully crafted Mother's Day present from a young child being unceremoniously dropped into the recycling bin. But minimalism is about focusing on what's important. If maintaining that link with the past is important to you, then you'll find a way to incorporate those touchstones into your current life. After all, minimalism isn't about making sure that the number of possessions we own is kept to some magical low number; it's about ensuring that we live with intentionality and that we uphold the values we believe in.

However, if this aspect of minimalism is a deal-breaker for you, ask yourself where items of sentimental value fit into your life right now. Are they put in pride of place in your home? Or are they tucked away in storage boxes, out of sight (perhaps out of mind?), and possibly contributing to the clutter problem in your home?

....

Clearing the decks is important, particularly in our everyday lives. The proliferation of clutter in our homes has sparked a mini boom in tidying specialists who are shown on TV going into people's homes and ruthlessly corralling their possessions into piles marked Keep, Donate, Dump. No doubt you've experienced yourself the satisfaction of clearing out a wardrobe that's been subsumed by clothes you haven't seen, let alone worn, in years, or a spare room that's teeming with decades-old newspapers, trophies from long-forgotten sports events, or manuals for appliances that stopped working years ago. It can be a remarkable process, one that frees up space in your living environment and leaves you feeling lighter, unencumbered by life's detritus.

In the end, minimalism is about figuring out what makes you truly happy and keeping only those things – and those concepts and people – around you that make you happy, and that contribute to your life. Many of the above myths illustrate the cultural hold that the act of acquiring things has over our mind-set in the 21st century; the extent to which we invest aspects of ourselves in the possessions we own, instead of seeing objects for what they are: tools to serve us.

TURNING THE TIDE

The problem for many of us is a practical one: the enormous tide of objects that sweeps into our homes. One way to stem this apparently unstoppable tsunami is to simply opt out of bringing so many items into our homes, heading off the tide at the pass.

Over the course of a century, we've gone from living relatively simple lives to finding ourselves at the nexus of vast transcontinental trading routes, no matter where in the world we happen to live. Thanks to the Internet and to highly evolved supply chains, each of us can purchase and have shipped to us almost anything, from almost anywhere in the world. This is in contrast to our grandparents' time, when people often spent entire lifetimes building up a beloved collection of possessions.

In 1930, the average American woman owned nine outfits. The equivalent figure for today is 30.

The same woman would have spent years collecting items for her 'bottom drawer,' the figurative home for items such as sheets and other traditional household goods that, as a newlywed, she'd be expected to bring to her marital home. With incomes on a much lower footing than today, and with fewer shops to browse in, personal possessions were treasured and carefully tended to, often over the course of a lifetime – or, in the case of family heirlooms, over a number of lifetimes.

Now, in an age when Amazon can deliver a package to your door, when you can source jewelry or clothing from the other side of the world for just a few dollars, or stock up on cheap electronics at your local supermarket, it's difficult to invest much innate worth in each item that enters the home. It's easy, however, to accrue a lifetime's worth of 'stuff' in just a few years, or even months.

As Annie Leonard, executive director of Greenpeace USA, has said in the past, for a large proportion of the Western world 'there is no longer an economic obstacle to having the illusion of luxury.'[1]

Meanwhile, although the act of embarking on a declutter can be liberating for the person witnessing their closets and rooms being reclaimed by space, decluttering creates the problem of what to do with the items you've collected; whether to dump them in your city's waste stream, recycle them, or donate them to charity.

In this age of greater environmental awareness, we're all familiar with the jolt of failure and disappointment that hits us when we place bags of trash out for collection as the garbage truck makes its rounds. So the option of bringing bags of once-loved sweaters and too-tight pantsuits to our local charity shop comes as a sweet release from the incipient guilt of adding to the world's landfill problem.

In some instances, a classic coat or a cleverly designed dress can go on to live another life. It may go to a new owner who has mastered the trick of hunting down bargains in charity shops or flea markets. But a large proportion of charity shop stock goes unsold and ends up being shipped to the developing world, where it becomes subsumed in an already saturated clothing market. (According to UN figures for 2013, the USA exported $687 million worth of used clothing, including $55 million to Guatemala, $23 million to Tanzania, and $21 million to Angola; meanwhile, the UK exported $612 million worth of worn clothes, including $65 million worth to Ghana and $42 million worth to Kenya.)[2] The net result is often that clothing prices in the developing world are driven down, putting added pressure on local manufacturers to compete.

Recycling also has its problems. In the area of clothing, just 1 percent of textiles are recycled back into textiles every year.[3] In addition, in 2018 public waste authorities across the Western world were thrown into a panic by China's decision to radically reduce the quantity of recyclable plastic it had previously been processing. The message was clear: Waste has never simply disappeared, but the long-standing get-out clause consumers once had, of diverting items to 'recycling,' is becoming a less reliable course of action. Ultimately, recycling is only ever a back-end solution to a problem that should have been tackled years, if not decades, ago.

THE STUFF STOPS HERE

The truth is that while decluttering can induce a wonderful feeling, we'll only see lasting change in our surroundings if we change our buying habits, the habits that introduce so much stuff to our homes in the first place.

The most productive new habit we can form is... doing nothing. That is, the habit of not shopping for clothes, toys, or gadgets, and so reducing the number of items we bring into our homes every year. Cutting down on the number of tank tops we acquire every season, asking relatives not to give our children plastic toys as gifts, holding off for another year before upgrading a smartphone – all of these actions would go some way toward preventing the accumulation of stuff in our homes and, if replicated across the board, would begin to chip away at demand for such items.

After all, it's only because we, as consumers, create a demand for consumer goods that clothes, plastics, and electronics are available to us in such vast quantities. More than 2 billion people across the world own smartphones, and more than 7 billion smartphones have been made since the iPhone made its debut in 2007.[4] In the USA, the average smartphone ends up being in use for just two years, not because it stops working but because its owner is persuaded to upgrade to the latest model. According to Greenpeace USA, at this rate of consumption the average US citizen is likely to own 29 handsets over the course of their lifetime.

Clearly, this level of consumption, in terms of the use of the Earth's resources, is almost impossible to sustain at the rate we're going. So, in terms of a fresh definition of materialism, it can be useful to consider which items we really need to buy.

Sociologist and economist Juliet Schor has urged consumers to engage in true materialism – that is, the recognition of the innate value of individual material goods.[5] She's theorized that we'd be less inclined to junk smartphones and clothes and toys as frequently as we do if we appreciated the craftsmanship that went into making them, and noted the material resources that were harvested to manufacture them.

Mass production has meant that we've lost some of the respect with which we once regarded good workmanship.

It means that we can sometimes fail to appreciate that almost every item that comes into our possession by way of the retail process has been the culmination of effort and labor, whether it's in mining, manufacturing, transport, marketing, or product development. Restoring some of this respect to the process may, Schor argues, result in us slowing down our now customary churn through successive generations of the latest smartphones.

Ultimately, as we become more conscious of the environment, we have the choice to either maintain our planet's current level of consumption or, on an individual basis, rein things in. Large-scale issues like the depletion of natural resources, or the problematic nature of the disposal of the consumer goods we purchase, can feel too big to tackle head-on. But striking a blow against mindless consumerism in one's own life can feel empowering. And if enough people make an effort to do so, who knows what wider positive effects will be unleashed.

RELATIVE VALUES

So, minimalism is about being intentional about what you allow into your life, thinking about what should be there, and perhaps saying goodbye to certain objects (or people) that no longer belong. However, it's less about the absence of things, and more about bringing intentionality into your thinking and into your actions, devising a system of mindfulness for how you choose the things around you.

In fact, minimalism is about readjusting your mind-set. It's about liberating the mental space required to implement new habits and freeing up the bandwidth required to consider new choices and the exciting challenges about to enter your life.

But first you need to determine which potential challenges most excite you. What opportunities would you love to have offered to you? What do they look like? Why do they appeal to you? How would they affect your life for the better?

Perhaps you'd love a promotion at work, or you'd prefer to switch jobs altogether and move into a field you find more fulfilling. What would that look like? Why would that particular new position make you happier? Do you think you could run your department or project more efficiently if you felt more devoted to your job? Would the job in a completely new industry draw on untapped talents you've been harboring for years?

Perhaps you dream of moving house and creating a new life for yourself and your family. What need within you would that fulfill?

Is your goal in life to raise a family? Is it to ensure that your family is raised in a secure, loving environment, with your children instilled with values that will see them through life?

Is your goal to concentrate on your career? To be of service to others and to leave a body of work that will live long after you've shuffled off this mortal coil?

Is your goal to consolidate your life with your partner? To build a life together that you can both enjoy and look back on with pride?

But perhaps you think you're quite content with your lot in life. Or perhaps you feel that you're not the kind of person who strives for goals, that career achievements – well, they simply aren't for you. Author Greg McKeown has an uncomfortable truth that you need to hear: 'If you don't prioritize your life, someone else will.'[6] It underlines the reality that too many of us find ourselves working in jobs that we should have left years ago, or labor away in roles – to provide for growing families, for example – that no longer serve us or fulfill us in any real way.

You'll notice that right at the heart of these goals are people: your family, your partner, or yourself. Sometimes it's easy to confuse the trappings of conventional success for real and lasting improvements to your life or the lives of your loved ones. As minimalism helps us clear clutter from our lives, we make room for what really matters: our goals and the people who mean the most to us.

What will help you in your path toward achieving a minimalist lifestyle is to remember that the emphasis must be on people, not things.

Ultimately, one of the most powerful actions we can decide to take is to divine our own true goals in life. So look into your soul, and find out what you truly want to do with 'your one wild and precious life,' as poet Mary Oliver once termed it.[7]

When our goals align with our values – when a love of the energy and creativity of young children can be combined with a goal of starting a family, when a belief in the merits of hard work can be channeled into building your career, when loyalty and good humor can be directed toward creating a mutually fulfilling life with a partner – the force that's unleashed can be unstoppable. When we form goals that are out of sync with our values, however, it becomes that bit harder to achieve progress.

So the process of finding your life goals, underpinned by your values, is critically important. After all, it'll determine many of your actions in the years ahead, and it'll help you determine which tasks are essential and which actions must be jettisoned for the sake of achieving your goals.

Decide what matters most

Knowing what you want out of life can help inspire you to clear away the objects in your path.

1. Define your goals

Survey your life as it currently stands. What are the objects or activities that serve a useful purpose and most help you in your journey toward your goals? What are the relationships that most enrich your life? More to the point, what are the objects, activities, or relationships that neither help you in your progress toward your goals nor enrich your life? These should be discarded.

2. Identify what brings value

Looking at your values, at the core qualities that you believe serve you best as a person, as a partner, as a parent, as a member of society, where do you want to go and what do you want to achieve with your life? Perhaps you have strength, intelligence, kindness, or an unshakable faith. Write these down, including as much detail as you can about what success would look like to you.

3. Determine how you spend your time, money, and energy

Time, money, and energy are all resources that we have at our disposal. Remember that the areas in which we invest these resources will then continue to grow. If you neglect to invest in key areas of your life, such as your goals, those aspects of your life will fail to thrive. If you don't remove aspects of your life that aren't aligned to your goals or your values, you're in danger of seeing these flourish instead, at the cost of what is really important to you.

....

Ultimately, it's your duty to yourself to focus on what you want in life, and to channel your energy into actions that will help you realize your most cherished goals. If creating a sustainable life with your partner is what matters most to you, let that be your priority. If moving your family to an area where your children can lead a lifestyle that will help them thrive is your goal, concentrate on that. If writing a novel that throws light on the modern condition is an ambition that's burnt in your soul for years, let that be your guiding light.

Finally, don't forget that your most essential duty is to your own well-being. It's easy to get carried away on the high of dispatching things that 'bring little value.' But don't forget that value comes in many forms. If an object or activity or relationship brings you true pleasure, it has value. Even if your grandparents' wedding pictures don't advance your cause toward a job promotion, they may very well be dear to you. While plodding along at the local park will never win you any medals for running, it may well be a source of quiet personal satisfaction after a week tied to your office desk. Minimalism is about doing without unnecessary baggage, but if you find that you're getting rid of things that you truly enjoy, then you're doing it wrong. After all, minimalism is about creating space in your life for joy and fulfillment, not snuffing these out where they already exist.

It's time to step into your future, one that's been cleared of clutter and the detritus of a life you don't want. It's time to create the life you've always wanted for yourself.

CHAPTER 1

HELP OUT YOUR HOME

The desire to live in a comfortable home must be one of the most basic and fundamental urges we have. Whether you live in a plush mansion or a tiny studio apartment, your home is your refuge, a place of safety that you return to after a day spent in the world at large. Our home gives us shelter and security, with its four walls providing a buffer against the often harsh world beyond. Each and every one of us wants to associate our home – the place we lay our heads at night – with peace, with a feeling of sanctuary, with a sense of belonging. It's a powerful feeling, knowing that somewhere on this Earth there's a special place, no matter how big or small, where you can be yourself and relax. It may be a cliché but home really is where the heart is, and it's only when our home has been taken away from us, or is under attack, that we fully understand its role in our psychological make-up.

Given that our home is our safe space, and we're inclined to spend as much time as possible there, it's natural that we invest much love and attention in making it as comfortable and aesthetically pleasing to us as possible. I still recall the pride with which I installed a cheap pair of scented candles in candlesticks on the dresser in the first room I rented. Nearly everything in that room was owned either by the landlord (the bed, the dresser, the chair) or had been given to me by my mother (the bed linen, the set of bath towels) and this was the very first decorative item I myself had bought. I felt like I was carving out a little space in the world that was truly mine – even if those candles ended up burning down to the wick long before my next paycheck.

I'd discovered the pleasure of buying an item of home decor and investing in myself as a person of good taste. I thought to myself, only a person with good taste would buy these candles, with their marbled pattern and lavender scent (rather sickly and overpowering, if I can be honest two decades later), to decorate their home, so by simply buying these candles, I could be a young woman with good taste!

Within a few months, my tiny rented room was chock-full of trinkets: incense for an incense burner I didn't yet own, earthenware wine goblets for the parties I never threw, and cheap vases for the flowers I couldn't afford to buy. All because I was a shy young woman who believed that she could buy 'good taste.'

The desire to stamp our own personality on
our surroundings is deeply ingrained.

I certainly loved the keepsakes that my mother had brought into her marriage. She'd curated her collection over a period of decades, and it was made up of much-loved gifts, carefully selected ornaments, and souvenirs, all of which meant the world to her. By contrast, I was able to accumulate piles of junk from the earliest opportunity, due to the 1990s boom in cheap consumer goods. Very soon, I had a lifetime's worth of 'souvenirs,' with only my recall of purchasing them in one particular discount store to anchor them in my memory.

PEER PRESSURE

It's easy to judge my younger self. But it highlights another fundamental truth about humans: the pride we take in our homes. Millions of dollars are spent on home improvements and home design every year. We feel that our homes are an outer expression of our inner character, and reflect qualities about us – refinement and good taste, for example. In its healthiest form, this impulse prompts us to keep our homes clean and to stay on top of large-scale house maintenance, reminding us that the brickwork needs re-pointing, that a couple of roof tiles may need attention, that the boiler should be checked before winter hits.

But in recent decades, particularly since the economic boom of the 1990s, this natural urge has found its expression in 'keeping up with the Joneses,' and there has been an ever-escalating war of attrition on any living space that may be considered less than perfect. We feel under pressure to have the most up-to-date kitchen, the most upscale waterfall shower in our bathroom, the very latest swing set on our patio. After all, didn't the Joneses down the road splash out on a designer kitchen not so long ago? Will we end up as the only house on the street without a kitchen island? Will this ultimately affect the price of our house?

I regularly see this in the neighborhood near my home. The homeowners have always been house-proud, taking delight in tending their verdant gardens and ensuring their two-up two-downs look at least as smart as the other similar houses on the street. But just a few years ago, I noticed the telltale sign of imminent renovation outside one or two of the houses: an empty dumpster parked in the driveway. As the days passed, the dumpster would fill up with the typical detritus of a rigorous refurbishment – rolls of linoleum flooring, yellow-colored cupboard doors accessorized with brushed-steel handles, all the relics of a home that had been lovingly kitted out decades before with the mod-cons of the mid-20th century. Over the weeks that followed, excitement would mount as fitters arrived to install sleek new kitchen cabinets painted some sophisticated gray, plumb the gas for the newest five-burner stove, and lay a flagstone floor.

Over the course of a couple of years, such renovation piles would appear outside more and more houses on the same street, this time filling up with household artifacts from the 1990s, or even the 2000s – the cupboard doors in 'country pine' with their wrought-iron handles, the granite-look Formica countertops – as families decided that their 20- or even 10-year-old kitchen was no longer cutting it in the design stakes and needed a makeover.

Were these people living in seriously substandard conditions, slaving away in relics of the past? Wearing their fingers to the bone as they laundered the family's clothes on a washboard over a bucket? Or did they see their neighbors' state-of-the-art kitchens and start looking at their own homes with new, freshly dissatisfied eyes?

It's only natural to want our homes to be as comfortable and as aesthetically pleasing as possible. But would these refurb-happy homeowners have been as anxious to throw away their 1990s kitchens if the Joneses down the street hadn't remodeled their pantry?

Is it possible that if they hadn't compared their lot
with the Joneses, it would never have occurred
to them to upgrade to the latest designs?

Just like my younger self buying scented candles because it seemed like something a young person should do, having the most up-to-date kitchen is, for many people, something that a modern family should do.

So just how much is updating our home a matter of ensuring that our family can lead their lives in a warm, safe environment, and how much is about trying to keep up with the Joneses?

The essential task of keeping one's family warm and sheltered is already achievable within the confines of the average kitchen, even if it doesn't have a five-burner stove. Notwithstanding the occasional malfunctioning fridge or oven, even the older kitchen serves the purpose of enabling a family to prepare and enjoy three meals per day.

What more could you possibly want from your kitchen?

Well, quite a bit, actually. Whether we're aware of it or not, sometimes our kitchens – or our whole homes, or simply our possessions – are turned into fashion statements or into pawns in our family's rivalry with the Joneses. Or they may be already so bound up with our own identity that other comparisons come into play, such as which schools our kids go to, or where we go on vacation.

OBJECTS OF DESIRE

It doesn't help that an entire industry has developed around the concept of making consumers feel they should buy more and more things, whether they need them or not. Marketing executives spend huge sums each year persuading us that the latest home sound system or television will make us more popular or more attractive to potential partners. In some respects advertising is just pushing an open door. The executives know that no lavish TV advertisement is as powerful as our own mental image of what it would be like to live in the 'perfect' home.

Back in the 19th century, philosopher and psychologist William James wrote about the extent to which humans identify with their material possessions. 'A man's self is the sum total of all that he can call his,' he wrote in 1890. 'Not only his body and his psychic powers, but his clothes and his house, his wife and his children, his ancestors and friends, his reputation and works, his lands and horses, and yacht and bank-account. All these things give him the same emotions. If they wax and prosper, he feels triumphant; if they dwindle and die away, he feels cast down.'[8]

Many of us have fallen into this trap. After all, we know the psychological effect of having our possessions removed from us. Studies of burglary victims note the extent to which people who have had their property stolen liken their experience to an attack on their identity or sense of self.[9]

Human beings are programmed to try to make sense of their world by attaching meaning to events and objects.

It's why we get so sentimental over our wedding photographs, the tickets from a concert by our favorite musician, or a humorous present from coworkers when we moved on from our first job. These things may have little monetary value but they may mean the world to us because they represent a relationship with a loved one, remind us of special experiences, or illustrate how far we've traveled in life.

This isn't a design fault in humans; it's something to be celebrated. Honed over thousands of years, our ability to invest objects with symbolic meaning has enabled us to create art. What is art, after all, if not a creative work that has meaning beyond its immediate and most obvious use? Leonardo da Vinci's *Mona Lisa* is more than an accomplished portrait: it represents the apotheosis of the maestro's skills and points to a high-water mark in Western civilization.

In our everyday lives, however, problems arise when we fail to discriminate between which objects are truly meaningful and which ones we're hanging on to – or hankering after – simply because they've become an outward expression of our own inner worth.

Society recognizes the power of
the items we call our own.

A key element of joining large, all-consuming institutions where we're required to subsume our personalities and bend our will to the command of others – say, in being inducted into military service or joining a religious order – is the forfeiting of our personal possessions in a maneuver designed to re-order our thinking. Even far back in history, the link with our possessions is strong: As archaeologists have shown, the ancient Egyptians, along with many other historical cultures, opted to bury their kings and queens with their personal possessions. As our possessions become incorporated into 'the extended self,'[10] they retain a certain power over us.

If objects retain a power over us by virtue of our ownership of them, shouldn't we be more discerning about which ones we bring into our lives? Are we not leaving ourselves open to disappointment or even psychological distress in the event of our objects being taken away from us, or of their being lost?

As the 20th-century psychoanalyst Erich Fromm mused, 'If I am what I have and if what I have is lost, who then am I?'[11] More than four decades on, his point is as pertinent as ever: Why construct one's sense of self on foundations as precarious as owning the latest sound system or a state-of-the-art kitchen?

Fromm's observation was made at the height of society's disenchantment with materialism, just as the counter-culture hippies of the 1960s were maturing into critics of capitalism. It also predated the phenomenon we witnessed from the 1990s onward, of consumer goods becoming cheaper and cheaper as production was outsourced to the developing world.

The observation also highlights an issue we need to face in our own homes: Should we attach the same level of meaning to a CD by a band we passingly admired a decade ago as we do to our child's first pair of shoes? To a photograph of our parents on their wedding day? And should you allow your dearest possessions, these emotional touchstones which represent milestones in your personal history, to be swamped by extraneous household items, useless paraphernalia that found its way into your home, or cheap junk that was bought on a whim?

Should you allow yourself to be inundated with
things that ultimately mean little to you?

It's time to make room for your future self, and for the life
that you really want. The good news is that the tools you
need are already within your grasp: the insight to look at your
life and decide what is really important, and the judgment to
know which items to recycle, sell, or throw out, as junk that's
weighing you down. All that's needed is the willpower to look
at your life with fresh eyes, and the determination to see this
task through.

CLUTTERED HOME, CLUTTERED MIND

According to one 2016 study, the presence of clutter in
our homes can affect our personal happiness. 'When
[clutter] becomes excessive, it can threaten to physically
and psychologically entrap a person in dysfunctional home
environments which contribute to personal distress and
feelings of displacement and alienation.'[12]

However, the urge to accumulate is strong. We may hang on
to things because they give us a sense of security. Or we may
be reluctant to part with our well-worn possessions because
they provide us with a sense of who we are in the world.
According to psychologists, the hoarder mentality sometimes

kicks in when we feel anxious or unsupported in our lives. We may not be able to control our circumstances, or how people treat us, but we can certainly maintain a sort of order by saving the cheap keepsakes we picked up on a trip to England decades ago, even if they're under a heap of keepsakes from every vacation we've taken since then.

This need to retain things may have been useful in the past, when retail supply chains weren't as highly evolved as they are today, back when useful tools were difficult to come by and cost a lot. But when almost every item of flat-pack furniture today includes an Allen key, there's little need to own a set of Allen keys in different sizes.

This practical impulse, to hang on to goods 'just in case,' sometimes extends beyond those items that are useful or even beautiful.

It can include clothes that no longer fit us, old children's toys, and books we haven't read in years.

However, the psychological cost of stockpiling possessions around us is high. It's difficult to unpick what's at play here, but psychology professor Stephanie Preston believes that we stockpile for the bad times we expect further down the road.

She conducted studies in which participants were socially rejected and noted the effect this had on their subsequent behavior. She found that they laid claim to more objects after experiencing social rejection. Bizarrely, they loaded up on practical items, like torches and backpacks.[13]

Another study suggests that people will make unhealthier food choices if they're in a cluttered environment.[14] In one experiment, researchers found that participants who had been put into a low-self-control mind-set were more likely to reach for cookies when placed in a kitchen that was messy and disorganized.

In addition, there's evidence that visual clutter may inhibit your ability to read the emotions of other members of your family. A 2016 study of moviegoers, and the effect of extraneous visual stimuli on their perception of the emotions being portrayed on-screen, showed that viewers found it difficult to interpret actors' non-verbal cues when the scene's background was cluttered.[15]

People report feeling 'imprisoned' and 'oppressed' by piles of books or large boxes of tableware that's never been used.

One 2010 study found that in couples who lived in homes characterized by extraneous stuff, levels of cortisol – a hormone associated with stress – tended to be high in the female partner in the relationship.

So, as well as being generally unsightly, clutter may make you unhappy, prompt you to eat more high-calorie foods, lead to greater family discord, and suffer from higher stress.

Clutter forms an obstruction to my goals for the day.

After all these years of living in a tiny apartment, if I wake up and realize that last night's dirty dishes are still in the kitchen sink – which is, after all, just temporary clutter – I feel a disincentive to get out of bed. Although they aren't physically in my way, the image of the encrusted saucepans or fat-splattered skillets will weigh on me, a reminder of a job from a previous day that's yet to be done.

My friend Paula talks about the frustration she feels when she glances at her bedroom dresser and her eye is caught by the melee of obsolete eye shadows and half-empty bottles of moisturizer that litter its surface. 'It's unsightly and puts me in a bad mood almost from the moment I get out of bed,' she says. 'Every few months, I try to come up with a system that will impose some order – right now I'm planning to buy a few of those clear plastic stands so that my lipsticks can be turned into a display – but the dresser always ends up returning to its natural state of disorder after a week or so, and I go back to feeling annoyed and disappointed in myself.'

Meanwhile, another friend Helen is amazed at her capacity for accumulating books she never reads. 'I used to read a lot, but although life has got a lot busier in recent years and I no longer have time to read, I still love to buy books. At this point, there's no room for them in the bookcase, and they're piling up beside my bed. I'm literally tripping over them.'

It's all too easy to reach a point where our possessions are actually getting in our way. In the initial years of creating a home, gathering a little collection of possessions is exciting. It marks our progression as an adult: the first set of mugs, the first piece of art. But all too soon, our enthusiasm for those little touches that make a home starts to become excessive.

If you live in a big house, you can perhaps hide the problem by packing up your excess books, CDs, and DVDs and placing them out of sight in a spare room. After all, they're still there. You can access them any time. They just won't be literally in your way any more.

The obvious solution is simply to dispose of the clutter, to ruthlessly cull the contents of our living spaces, to pull out the boxes of long-unplayed DVDs and consign them to the charity shop.

In many instances, clutter represents the end point of a process of procrastination.

For instance, why do I still have a leather jacket that I bought in 2008? It never truly fitted me, not even when I bought it over a decade ago, and it doesn't go with any of my other clothes. It's because every time I look at it and think about donating it to Oxfam, I think about how much it cost me, and about how maybe some day I'll finally have an outfit that it complements, and I begin to berate myself for even thinking about getting rid of it. Back into its hiding place in the wardrobe it goes, and the fateful day when I finally have to confront my feelings about this dumb jacket and make a decision over its future is put off for at least another few months.

WHY DECLUTTERING SEEMS DIFFICULT

Most of us have had that feeling of admiring our freshly decluttered wardrobe or cupboard, of the undeniable pleasure of knowing that everything is in its place, of a sensation of feeling lighter and freer as a result. So why can't we recall that feeling at will and be inspired to embark on similar challenges more frequently?

Lifestyle coach and author Kerri Richardson has an interesting take on the role of clutter. She believes that, on some subconscious level, we retain clutter in an attempt to avoid other important tasks, or to stall actions in our life journey that would otherwise further our goals. Our minds, fearful of the unknown, sabotage our efforts to implement this one change – a clear-out – that would give us the psychological boost we need to get on with a life-changing project, such as getting a new job or re-evaluating our relationships.

This would explain why we approach decluttering with such ambivalence: In our conscious minds, we're well aware of the short-term gain – satisfaction, a sensation of clarity and freedom, a return to order, the freeing-up of valuable storage space – but the task just seems too onerous, too daunting.

It's similar to the inner demons we encounter when we embark on other new projects that will benefit us in the long run. It's the insidious voice that trash-talks our efforts when we go for a run. It's the moment of self-doubt when we look at ourselves in our fitness gear as we prepare for a new gym class. It's the moment's hesitation before we sign up to a new dating app. But just as we know that joining the gym, and getting out and meeting new people, are good for us, deep down we know that clearing away the debris of our old lives is the best way of moving forward.

Clearing clutter is the best way of making room for you and your goals.

If clutter represents the build-up of decisions not taken, no wonder it feels uncomfortable to finally tackle those boxes of old diaries, the unwatched DVDs of movies now on Netflix, the warranties of appliances long since replaced.

And wouldn't it be wonderful to have that space returned to you? To repurpose all that room for the things you use in your life right now, rather than the life you used to have or the life you wish you had? Wouldn't it be nice to donate the sweaters that no longer fit you, and let them go to a person who will wear them and cherish them? Wouldn't you prefer to see your children's toys, which they outgrew long ago, go to a crèche or playgroup where they'll be appreciated all the time? Those books you once loved but haven't opened in years – wouldn't you like them to bring joy to someone browsing in your local charity shop?

MISSION POSSIBLE

The tidying expert Marie Kondo has become famous for her approach to clearing clutter. She urges anybody immersed in the challenge to take each of their possessions, hold it in their hands and ask: *Does it spark joy?*

In many ways, Kondo's method cuts to the heart of the challenge. It obliges us to ask instinctive questions about our relationship with the item. For those of us who worry that, if every garment was obliged to 'spark joy,' the contents of our workwear wardrobe would very quickly end up in the bags earmarked for the charity shop, it's worth modifying this system slightly.

Before you start the decluttering process, set the parameters. The aim isn't to turn your home into a sterile-looking box devoid of all personality and character; all you're doing is creating a space for you and your very best life: for your future. You're simply removing those elements that no longer work for you, and which no longer represent the real you. You're not obliterating your personal history.

So it stands to reason that certain essentials will be staying put. You may be anxious about personal items – a cherished family heirloom, say, or your favorite childhood book. If you feel a deep connection with these items, then it goes without saying that you should keep them. Remember: if you're getting rid of things that you truly enjoy, then you're doing it wrong. The good news is that determining which items truly give you joy is a simple process of listening to your intuition.

How to declutter

1. Decide on your plan of action

Don't make it your mission to declutter the entire basement or garage in an afternoon. Start with a small project, such as decluttering your desk, or a small element of a larger project, such as one corner of your garage. Focus on a defined area that's manageable within the time you have available.

2. Set a time limit

So, what period of time should you be prepared to give over to your task? Certainly don't devote an entire day to this endeavor. For one thing, the thought of spending a whole day sorting through the detritus of the past is enough to drain the joy out of anybody. Like clutter and physical space, jobs tend to expand to fit the time allocated to them.

Instead, set a limit of two hours to the task, with no more than three two-hour sessions a day, each separated by at least an hour's break. This way you'll work much more quickly and efficiently to complete it in that period. You'll also be more open to resuming the project at the earliest possible opportunity.

3. Begin decluttering!

Make space for four piles, which you're going to designate as 'Keep,' 'Donate,' 'Recycle,' and 'Trash.'

Starting at the top left-hand corner of the area being decluttered, remove each item and briskly ask yourself:

– *Have I used it within the last year?*

– *Would I buy it now if I saw it in a store?*

– *Do I have a 'home' for this item in my home?*

If the answer to at least one of the questions is 'Yes,' place it in the 'Keep' pile. For the rest of the items, make a call on whether they could go on to another owner by way of donation to a local charity shop (the 'Donate' pile); you may also choose to try selling them on eBay. Otherwise, earmark them for either the local recycling scheme ('Recycle') or – as a last resort – the kerbside garbage collection by your municipal authority ('Trash').

Work until the end of your planned time period, taking regular breaks if you're tackling a larger job.

....

Sounds simple, doesn't it?

It may be simple, but that doesn't mean it's easy. Each time you pick something up, you're asking questions of both the item – be it a well-thumbed school yearbook, a football jersey that's too small for you, or a box of old gadgets – and yourself. Perhaps the item represents a different time in your life – sometimes our clutter is a build-up of the material reminders of a past phase.

Decluttering is an opportunity to ground us in the present, to put us in touch with what we need – right here, right now.

Thanks to advice from my mother, I've found over the years that taking short 'sprints' of time to get any project done is very effective. To this day, she takes a very practical approach, saying, 'You'd be surprised what you can get done in half an hour.'

I take her at her word, so as I knuckle down to a task like decluttering, I set a timer for 30 minutes, ignoring all distractions until the alarm sounds. I take a break of three to five minutes, then get back to work for another 30 minutes, and so on. Even if I'm working up fresh enthusiasm for the project, I'll commit myself to no more than four such 30-minute 'sprints,' i.e. one two-hour session. If, during a sprint, I think of another chore that needs to be done, I simply take a note of it and get back to the job in hand.

This course of action is ideal for decluttering: Not only can decluttering be emotional work, but a large-scale clear out can involve lifting and carrying, so it can be physically tiring too. Return to the task when you're refreshed and you'll be able to commit yourself to another brace of 'sprints.'

I suggest scheduling a glass of crisp white wine (or your favorite nonalcoholic beverage) and perhaps catching up with an episode or two of your favorite TV show directly afterward, as a reward.

AVOIDING 'IFS' AND 'BUTS'

As you declutter, keep the following pointers in mind:

IT'S NOT A SENTIMENTAL JOURNEY

If you have a family, you may ask yourself: *What about the drawings my children made when they were younger? What about their favorite stuffed toy – the orange teddy bear my son wouldn't sleep without when he was little?* It would be inhuman to expect anybody to throw out their dearest keepsakes – but the emphasis here should be on the word 'dearest.' A much-loved soft toy is completely different from a random finger painting created on a rainy Wednesday afternoon. So why not curate a small storage box of memories for each child? This is where your child's old companion can live now that he's retired from active service, and where he can spark joyful memories in years to come.

Celebrate your child's talent on an ongoing basis by sticking their latest artwork to the fridge for a few days; for many young children, the real joy comes from the act of being creative, not from knowing that Mom or Dad are carefully collating every item they'll produce over the years. If you like, include in the memory box particularly notable pieces of art, but be judicious about which ones you hang on to beyond their few precious weeks in pride of place in the kitchen. Slip the rest into recycling. After all, the very best art curators know that less is more.

FIGHT THE 'JUST IN CASE' IMPULSE...

For many of us who grew up in homes where thrift was valued, there's a temptation to hang on to items that may save us money later on. We may find ourselves thinking, *I might need that Lonely Planet guide to London, or I might lose enough weight to fit into that dress once more; it would be a shame to get rid of it.* The truth is, by the time I'm motivated enough to lose 10 pounds, that dress will have gone out of fashion; and by the time I return to London, that old guidebook will be out of date. Better that they go to new owners now, while they can still be enjoyed, instead of sitting in my home, taking up space while waiting for an event that may never happen.

... BUT BRACE YOURSELF

Reconcile yourself to the fact that occasionally you'll indeed need a specific size of Allen key, one that's identical to the one you dispatched to the charity shop two or three years ago. I'd argue that the benefit you gained from the space liberated in your declutter outweighs the benefit of having a set of cheap tools close to hand. In any case, it's useful to have a quick rule of thumb for just such a scenario. Ask yourself: *If I were to throw out this item, then one day in the future I found that I needed it, would I be able to source a replacement over the course of a weekend for $20 or less?* If the answer is yes, let the item go.

So that biscuit tin full of Allen keys from the flat-pack cabinet I put together a few years ago? Send them to a charity shop. What about the cache of half-empty coral-colored nail polishes that I favor for my toes in the summertime? There are always dozens to choose from in the local drugstore. That snazzy turkey platter I bought on sale but never use because I hardly ever entertain? It's time to accept that it should go to a home where it'll see daylight.

EVERYTHING IN ITS PLACE

So, you've decided that you don't need four extra fitted sheets for every bed in the house, and that one set of pliers is plenty to have at hand. You've bagged up the items that will either travel to their new, temporary home at the local charity shop, or be recycled or dumped.

Mission accomplished, right? Well, no.

Whatever has been saved from the fate of being donated, recycled, or dumped must be either returned to its previous 'home' or assigned a new home and placed there.

A lot of the time, clutter is simply stuff that doesn't have a home. If that's the case, then create one. Has the drawer beside your kitchen sink become a rat's nest of wires, of charger cables bundled up with Ethernet cables? Then create two distinct bundles: one of cables that you use every day, the other of lesser-used wires (Ethernet cables, cables used to charge up camera batteries, and so on) in the other pile. I put the everyday cables into a bag that lives in the kitchen drawer; it means that whenever I need to charge my mobile phone, I know the relevant cable will be there. The important thing is to remember to return it to the drawer after you use it. For the other cables, I use stationery labels to identify which item they belong to, e.g. 'Bluetooth speaker charging cable,' and then I place them in a cheap cardboard storage box that I can salt away in the bottom of the living room dresser. Again, for those rare occasions when I need an Ethernet cable, I know exactly where to turn.

Encourage children to assign homes for their own possessions. It's inevitable that toys will spread out from children's bedrooms but try to persuade younger members of the family to take pride in both their surroundings and their possessions. Start them with the practice of collecting up their teddy bears, toy cars or Lego pieces in the evening as they prepare for bed, and either placing them in a shared toy box in the living area or in their own toy box in their bedrooms. Ultimately, however, remember that children only act in line with the behavior modeled by the adults in their lives, so if you've been failing in this task, expect children to complain that it's too big an ask.

If you find that items that have been allocated a home are still mysteriously migrating from place to place, you need to address the reason. Perhaps the home you've assigned to them isn't suitable or you need a new system. I thought I'd cracked my filing problems when I decided that a small ledge in the hallway of my apartment would be the perfect place to temporarily store letters, bills, supermarket offers, and contractors' flyers that came through the letterbox. It wasn't: the narrow shelf was already home to my keys, my wallet, my gym entry card…. Very quickly, the shelf would become overburdened and incoming letters would find their way back to old clutter magnets such as the coffee table, bookshelves, armchairs. The ledge simply wasn't fit for purpose. It didn't help that my filing was infrequent, leading to a build-up of mail at a location that hit its capacity all too easily. In the end, what was needed was systematically bringing all mail into the kitchen where it could be sorted daily into 'further action required' (e.g. bills), 'to be filed for further reference,' 'for recycling,' and 'for shredding.' It put an end to stray postal items taking up residence on any random flat surface.

Sometimes the secret to stopping clutter is simply an issue of location, location, location. The paper shredder that you hardly ever use? Try moving it from its current location (behind the futon in the spare room, still in its original box) to the cupboard beside the recycling bin. After all, you probably bought it in order to shred old credit card bills before recycling them, so why leave it hidden away in a corner of the home that you never use?

If, during decluttering, you come across an item of sentimental value that you struggle to find a home for, why not turn it into a point of interest or a work of art in your home? The typical minimalist look is often derided as being free of personality and individuality, but that's not accurate. There's always room for a much-cherished family heirloom, but why not give it space to 'breathe' – on a dresser or hung on a wall – instead of letting it be subsumed by worthless clutter?

MAKE DECLUTTERING PART OF YOUR LIFESTYLE

The process of reviewing your possessions should be an ongoing one, so that you regularly weigh up whether they should remain in your life. (Perhaps this is something you could tackle before you go on your summer vacation.) Each time you pick up one of the material items in your possession, it should prompt a fresh consideration of the role it plays in your life, and whether you still want or need it. If done right, this can be a regular source of pride at what you've accomplished in your life, how far you have come. But it's fundamentally about creating intentionality about the possessions you own and the material goods you wish to bring into your life.

Think about owning only those items
that mean something to you; that either
work for you or bring you joy.

They don't have to mean the world to you, but they're items that make your life a little richer for being in it.

If owning things with a sense of intentionality is the goal of keeping clutter under control, the flipside is hanging on to material goods that mean little or nothing to us. In its most insidious and harmful form, this can lead to hoarding, where people metaphorically drown in a sea of junk. But even long before that toxic end point, it's very easy to fall into the trap of consuming unthinkingly, or holding on to relics of the past.

If that doesn't give you pause for thought, consider this: If you don't make these decisions about your material goods, somebody else eventually will, possibly after your death, when you'll have no say over the fate of your most precious possessions. If you love your family, do them a kindness and embark on a declutter now. By regularly reviewing your possessions, winnowing out what is of little personal significance, you'll be consciously curating a collection of items that you love and that have a particular meaning for you, not unconsciously gathering mounds of old newspapers and dusty mementos that your surviving relatives may feel obliged to sift through before deciding their fate. By decluttering from time to time, and fully evaluating each object's place in your life, your relatives will be able to assume that everything you've kept is important, making their decisions easier.

If you're keeping an item out of consideration for somebody else and not for yourself – a potential heirloom for your children, say – have a conversation with them and see if they would like to accept the heirloom soon, instead of years from now. Don't waste any more time living a life that no longer belongs to you. You're never too old to start living the life you always wanted, in a fresher, brighter new setting.

Of course, one way to stop clutter building up in your home is to address the issue before items even come into it, and to simply avoid accumulating so much stuff. After undergoing the decluttering process and bringing a spirit of intentionality into your relationship with your existing possessions, it makes sense that any new possessions should be acquired only with the same mind-set, so try to buy only those goods that will bring value to your life or will hold a significance to you or your family.

THE COST OF CLUTTER

In the developed world our possessions are now so numerous that an entire industry has grown out of the necessity to contain them all. In the USA, the self-storage sector is worth $24 billion.[16] Given that the average US household now owns 300,000 items,[17] it's not surprising that we're having difficulty containing all our things in our own homes. And the problem isn't confined to the USA. In the UK, you'll find almost 45 million sq ft of storage space.[18]

The escalation of storage-space providers tracked the boom in cheap consumer products as manufacturing moved from high-cost labor economies to countries in the developing world. Confronted with a flood of cheap electronics and household items, homeowners embraced the choice and stocked up. Prices across the board fell further.

Take televisions. Until the 1980s, buying a television called for much thought and consideration. After all, television sets were expensive: a new TV cost about $300 in 1972, when the median income of families in the USA was $11,120.[19] Today, when the median household income in the USA is a shade more than $60,000, you can buy a 55in smart TV for... $300. It's no wonder, then, that homes often have more than one set, or that our TVs are upgraded on a more regular basis than they were just 20 years ago.

The trend extended right the way through the average modern family home. Where once we had just enough teacups to cater for the immediate family and a handful of callers, now we had entire cupboards-full of novelty mugs, teetering piles of Tupperware, and drawers full of rarely used kitchen implements (my own nadir was the purchase of a melon baller – years before I could afford to buy an apartment).

As production costs have fallen further still, the supply of household goods has increased dramatically – leading to the 300,000 individual items amassed by the average US household, for example. Meanwhile, US homes have increased in scale, with the size of the average home having tripled over the past 50 years. The US Department of Energy has estimated that a quarter of US households with two-car garages don't park their cars inside because the space is being used for storage.[20] We're effectively building bigger houses simply to accommodate our ever-increasing collections of possessions.

And what effect is this having on the environment? Annie Leonard has argued that the unprecedented level of goods production exacts too high a price from the Earth. In her 2009 movie *The Story of Stuff*, the Greenpeace USA executive director sets out her argument that low price tags on cheap electronic goods, for example, mask the environmental cost of mining the Earth for resources and of disposing of a cheap music-player, say, at the end of its life (which may come about not because it's stopped functioning but simply because its owner feels like an upgrade). Then there's the economic damage to the developing world by manufacturing items there at such low costs.

Every item produced during this extraordinary age of consumerism, which got underway in the last century, has to be disposed of at some point. Some of these items will decompose into organic matter or may be recycled into other goods, but a huge proportion will simply sit motionless under its own weight, long after its working life is over. And it's we who are fueling this tide of consumer goods, with our demand for personal electronic gadgets, cheap household goods, and cheaper clothes, too.

KEEP IT OUT!

So, there are many sound personal and environmental reasons to fight the urge to repopulate your newly streamlined, clutter-free living space with stuff. That's not to say it's easy to fight the forces of marketing and peer pressure, including our innate need to surround ourselves with possessions that will signal to our neighbors what exquisite taste we have. However, with a little determination and a few ground rules in your back pocket, you can help prevent the build-up of stuff in your own home by bearing a few of these guidelines in mind as you go about your day:

1. HOW LIKELY ARE YOU TO USE IT?

We've all been there: It's payday, you're in your favorite department store, and you see a canteen of high-end cutlery. It's true that you have a full complement of knives and forks at home, but wouldn't those fish knives look impressive at your next dinner party...?

Snap out of it! If a new purchase is going to end up being put aside in your home, being stored away for some indeterminate date in the future, it's more than halfway to becoming clutter. We have a natural instinct to collect things – things that will make our lives easier – but sometimes they only get swallowed up by the mountain of things we already have. You may think you're being prudent by stocking up on cheap smartphone charging cables ('Now,' you think, 'I'll always have a phone charger to hand – I'll never have to go looking for a cable!'), but inevitably the 'spare' charging cables simply disappear amongst everything else. Somehow, we manage to take more care of our stuff when it's a finite resource.

2. WHERE WILL IT LIVE?

An essential element of your decluttering exercise was asking yourself of every object: *Do I have a home for it?* So before you bring something new into the home, it's useful to consider its role in your house or apartment right now (not in the future, not 'If I had the perfect life,' but right now) and where this means you'll keep it. Where will it live in order to fulfill its purpose?

I'm lucky, I suppose, in that I live in a small apartment, and every purchase has to be carefully worked out: If I buy a new chair, an old chair is going to have to make way for it. But forget anything as grandiose as a chair; I don't have room on my bathroom shelf for so much as a new jar of moisturizer. Everything has to work for me within the space available. A friend operates a 'one in, one out' system. She'll only acquire something new on the condition that she gets rid of something else. It means she has to carefully consider every purchase and decide which of her current possessions should be either donated to charity or go on eBay.

3. IS IT REALLY A BARGAIN?

I met a friend recently and I could see from her shopping bags that she'd been in the city's largest budget store. Moreover, I could see from the look of glee on her face that she'd picked up a bargain. 'Go on,' I urged her. 'Let's see what you got.' With a flourish, she pulled out four sweaters, identical apart from their color. 'Two for the price of one!' she grinned. 'An absolute bargain!' Well, yes. Except that one of them was in a mustard-yellow shade that didn't suit her at all. I have a strong feeling that it'll soon become a white elephant in her wardrobe, and something else to be eventually thrown out. It's worth remembering that a bargain is only a bargain if you genuinely need the thing on sale. If it's simply going to go unworn and unloved, you've bought nothing more than clutter.

Occasionally, this rule has to be enforced even when we're not shopping – say, when friends or family members are trying to resolve their own clutter problem by giving items away to us. It goes against the grain for many of us who grew up in families where thrift was prized, but sometimes one person's clutter is also another person's clutter. Tell them you really appreciate the thought but that you simply don't have space for it. Perhaps suggest someone else you both know who would gladly accept it.

MAKING ROOM FOR YOUR LIFE

The 19th-century British designer William Morris, who helped found the Arts and Crafts Movement in the late 18th and early 19th centuries, once wrote, 'Have nothing in your house that you do not know to be useful or believe to be beautiful.' It's a dictum that serves us well more than a century later. For a minimalist, every item in the home must earn its keep. It must either contribute something to one's life or bring considerable joy.

There's something very appealing about living your life in surroundings where everything plays a role. Although the thought of a thorough declutter can be intimidating, think about the space that will be restored to you. Think about your most precious possessions emerging from under the tide of junk and finally finding a place in your life. When absolutely everything is kept, however, nothing can thrive.

If you're having difficulty getting started, remember to ask yourself: *How is this mountain of stuff helping me progress toward my goals in life?* More often than not, old, out-of-date items that have been salted away in your home only serve to weigh you down; they either get in your way physically or chip away at any sense of initiative that you have. Take control of the situation by embarking on a declutter of any size, even if it's only one shelf or wardrobe. Remember to ask yourself:

What brings value to my life? And keep only those items which serve you well or which you love.

And as you go into the future, make a promise to yourself that whatever comes into your home will be brought in because of its purpose in your life, not simply because it's the latest gadget or because everybody you know has one like it. Let the possessions you surround yourself with be of service to you personally, whether it's on a practical basis or because it holds a particular meaning for you.

There's a peace to be found when you feel a connection with the place where you lay your head every night. Knowing that you've an organic connection with all of your belongings – that you carefully selected that particular armchair before bringing it into your house, that the cutlery you use every day is the same set that your mother used when you were a child – gives you a powerful sense of being 'at home.' And all that's needed to accomplish this feeling is to remove the unnecessary excess surrounding you, to commit to being thoughtful and purposeful in your purchasing habits, and to leave room for intentionality in your life.

CHAPTER 2

WORK SMARTER, NOT HARDER

If our home is the sanctuary from which we venture forth each morning, work is where we take on the world for eight hours a day in order to put food on the table. Given that we spend so much time at work, it inevitably becomes an important element of our lives. It goes further than the mathematics of how we carve up our time. What we do to earn a crust can form a key part of our identity. Studies show that working also gives us a psychological boost: Going to work connects us with the world beyond the four walls of our home, it enhances our overall well-being, and we feel a sense of achievement from a job well done. Some go even further: 'Work gives you meaning and purpose and life is empty without it,' the late physicist Stephen Hawking would tell his children.

But in recent years, many people have battled the feeling that we were sold a lie. We grew up in a world where the message was clear: Study hard, get a good job, save up for a house, and you'll have a good life. After all, that was the route that had paid dividends for our parents' generation in the 1950s, 60s, and 70s. But what nobody could have foreseen was the world economy hitting a brick wall in the late 2000s, rewriting the life-plans of millions of twenty-, thirty- and fortysomethings in countries across the world.

Whereas our parents saw their efforts rewarded with the security of home ownership, healthy savings accounts, and the prospect of a gilded future, the steady rise of the stock market over the last decades of the 20th century and the last gasp of a pension system that guaranteed set payouts meant that by 2008 people who should have been in their prime earning years were facing the very real possibility of having their financial lives up-ended and destroyed. For those of us who saw our dreams of owning our own home, or starting our own families, or enjoying a fulfilling career go up in flames in the months and years that followed, it felt like the tearing-up of a contract we'd naively signed, the breaking of a promise that had been made to us years before.

Work had been billed as an arena where, for a substantial proportion of our lives, we'd be able to trade our labor in exchange for financial opportunities and security. The years of the Great Recession showed just how hollow that promise had been, and it prompted a rethink for many on the role work should play in our lives.

More than a decade on, the trauma of those years continues to have ramifications. In many industries wages have stagnated, or in real terms have even fallen. Meanwhile, employers make more and more demands of employees in terms of time and flexibility. Workers are expected to be available to respond to email outside working hours, and there's an assumption that they'll take on the responsibilities of co-workers who are sick or on leave. Over the same period, workers have seen their conditions eroded: Job security is a thing of the past, and once standard features of employment, such as pension plans and health insurance, are either non-existent or have been restructured to the point of being of practically no benefit to the recipients.

Is it any wonder that more and more of us
are rethinking our relationship with work?

On the one hand, as humans, the need to work is hardwired into us. We thrive when we're putting our talents to good use and when we truly feel we're making a difference. Studies show that we live longer, healthier lives when we feel a sense of purpose.[21] But the old model of work, the one handed down to us, the one that assumes we'll continue at any cost to our personal lives, is simply no longer fit for purpose.

MAKE IT PERSONAL

If one of the main aims of the minimalist lifestyle is to bring intentionality into one's life, doesn't it make sense that we'd seek greater purpose and meaning in a part of life that consumes so much of our time? So, having applied the principles of intentionality to your home, perhaps it's time to run the same rule over your work life.

Is there 'clutter' in your work life that's using too much of your time and energy? Is there unnecessary excess that's leaving too little room for intentionality? Are you getting distracted from the point of your role? Is your job distracting you from your commitment to yourself – to leading a life that's characterized by integrity and by devotion to finding your true passion?

The answer isn't to simply quit one's job or to take the decision to implement a self-styled 'go-slow.' The answer is to ask vital questions about your values and then look closely at how your current role aligns with them, and how it brings you closer to your goals.

Weighing up your own personal values and how they relate to your job may seem a bit too self-indulgent for something that is, after all, only supposed to pay the bills. But all too often people end up in jobs that have little to do with very fundamental beliefs they have about the world. Take the fund manager whose duties facilitate the flow of money into the fracking industry, even though she's an ardent environmentalist. Or the junior lawyer whose law firm assigns him to defend a wife-beater. Or the teacher who feels under pressure to educate his teenage pupils on a set of beliefs that he simply doesn't hold.

Nearly all jobs involve occasions where we face ethical dilemmas from time to time, but struggles with our conscience shouldn't be on our daily to-do list. Perhaps your company is a prominent donor to a political party or cause that you disapprove of. Or perhaps your employers have been slow to promote people from minority backgrounds, or they place undue pressure on working mothers. Or perhaps the everyday culture of your workplace is too tolerant of low-level sexism and racism. Sure, you can handle it – but think about how exhausting it is to have to deal, on a daily basis, with the knowledge that your employer harbors beliefs that are fundamentally different from your own.

The situation that's most likely to chip away at your happiness and hopes of self-fulfillment is the one in which your values aren't upheld by your work, even if your job is financially or intellectually rewarding. Or where your own values have changed over time, but the values of your company haven't.

It can be a bewildering process, gradually falling out of step with everything we once believed in. Career goals become meaningless. Rousing, round-robin emails from management become incomprehensible. Overly long meetings, whose purpose seems only to lengthen the working day, become unbearable.

Work, it seems, is more than a
way of just paying the bills.

Successive studies have shown that leading a life that has purpose and meaning results in a life that's longer and healthier. That feeling may come neither from the nature of your work nor even the status of your job. It flows from feeling that we're contributing to something that's greater than ourselves. One 2001 study found that hospital cleaning staff – who work in physically unpleasant conditions, often under great stress – reported that they derived greater satisfaction from their work when they framed their jobs as playing an essential role in the care received by patients.[22] The staff who were happiest didn't see themselves as engaged in degrading work, or work that's not valued by society; instead they saw themselves as vital in helping the hospital run more smoothly, in the fight against infection, and in getting patients home to their families again.

Can you summon up that level of engagement with your current role? Can you appreciate that you're contributing to a cause that's greater than yourself? Can you clearly see how your current job chimes with the values you cherish? Even better if all three come together – the result can be outstanding success. When your values are in line with your work life, when your values align with those of your employer, and when your career fuels your personal passion, the synergy that's released can make you unstoppable. As billionaire Warren Buffett noted, 'In the world of business, the people who are most successful are those who are doing what they love.'[23]

Dispelling the dissonance between your values and your job means clearing away clutter from that area of your life where you engage with the world beyond your home. When you clear away the clutter – in other words, the energy expended in justifying your work life to yourself – what's left is clarity of purpose and the opportunity to live this area of your life with intentionality. When you clear away the clutter, you free up the mental space to determine your passion and your calling. When you clear away the clutter, you can decide for yourself what true success looks like, and how you can set a course for it.

FOCUS ON YOUR FUTURE

When you look into the future and try to envisage what 'success' will look like, what do you see? Is it a corner office, with a large expense account and all the trappings of a high-octane career? Or is it taking ownership of a particular project at work, being given free rein to finally set things to rights, and getting the credit for making it a success? Or does your vision of success see you in a different field altogether, working on your passion?

Your values, your vision of success, your
passion in life are big considerations.

They can seem too big to be relevant to our day-to-day lives. After all, having to pin down your 'passion' is a potentially intimidating task: *What if I make a mistake? What should a 'passion' look like?* If 'passion' feels like too big, too weighty a word, ask yourself: *What gives me energy? What makes me enthusiastic at the thought of doing it?* (Oprah Winfrey has termed this sense of passion one's 'calling,' noting that it's how 'you become most truly alive.')

But these questions about values, success, and one's passion keep us on track as we pursue our goals. And they focus our minds on finding opportunities that will allow us to take the next step toward our ultimate goal, to lead a satisfying life. And by applying them regularly to our working lives, we can make things simpler for ourselves by ensuring that the path between our present and our most fulfilling future remains clear.

When we fail to identify our passion, when we grow complacent about our goals, it's all too easy for our talents and energies to be bundled up and used to fuel somebody else's ambition. You may not value your input or worth at work, but your employer certainly does. After all, why is the department tasked with meeting your needs called human resources? This is why finding your own passion is so important.

Yuval Noah Harari, author of *Sapiens*, has said that the key to surviving and thriving in the world of 2050 will be the skill of reinventing oneself. Over the past 20 years many of us have seen our work roles change, sometimes beyond all recognition, thanks to developments in technology or due to economic necessity. My own background is journalism, which has been completely transformed since the 1990s when I was a young reporter. Back then, I had one deadline per week; nowadays reporters file copy on a continuous basis throughout the working week. In the 1990s, newspapers had copyeditors and proofreaders who would look over news stories and serve as another pair of eyes in the production process; today, staff cuts at media organizations mean that the number of people who check a story before it hits the streets – or readers' smartphones – may be a lot smaller, and they'll likely be working on more stories. And that's to take the example of just one established profession. People who work in other fields report similar experiences: doctors bogged down with patient paperwork, bookkeepers who must be proficient at using accounting software, the mechanic whose wrench has been replaced by a powerful computer that can diagnose a car's faults.

Ultimately, a confluence of a number of factors – advances in technology, greater job mobility, and employers' expectations in relation to workers' ongoing professional development – mean that almost everybody who is working today can expect a shift of their terrain in the years to come.

It's easy to view uncertainty in the most negative terms. Many of us crave security and no unwelcome surprises on the road ahead of us. But what if this exciting new terra incognita is where you'll develop new skills and discover hidden qualities about yourself? What if the unfamiliar lands that are just out of sight are where you'll truly bloom?

The ability to be alert to what may be coming down the track, to adjust to new surroundings and to be open to new opportunities that will help us to achieve our goals, will be among the most useful skills we can develop. Nobody can predict the unknown, but anybody can prepare for whatever the future holds by upskilling, by keeping up to date on developments in the field they work in, and by always being prepared to avail themselves of whatever lucky break comes their way.

Even if you feel that you're not a strident go-getter, or that high-powered careers are only for other people, the truth remains that by virtue of being a human – with a human's amazing capacity for solving problems and taking a creative approach to work – you're already considered a resource. So why not get that resource working not just for your employer – but for you too?

Ask yourself: *Should my future – my well-being in the years to come – be bundled in with the obligations and duties I carry around in work?* The truth is that crafting the future you really want must be your priority.

MAKING THE CHANGE

But with only so many hours in the day, how can you effect change in your life without compromising either your home life or your work? You already work hard – but is it possible to work smarter? Is it possible to optimize the time you spend at work, so that you can devote more time to your driving passion?

First of all, how do you currently carve up your time? Are you treating time like the precious resource it truly is?

TAKE CONTROL OF YOUR TIME

Over the years, I've found that the most productive way to achieve progress is to have a broad structure for the day ahead – earmarking certain parts of the working day for certain elements of my workload, all the while ensuring there's enough wiggle room for the curveballs that life inevitably throws us. So, last thing at night, I'll look at my diary – where I've already noted appointments, deadlines, and tasks that are specific to the following day – and I'll jot down in my notebook, under the day's date, a list of the appointments and deadlines in the order in which they fall. Then, alongside, I'll write down my other tasks for the day, prioritizing the most important obligations.

It's a simple step but it gives a structure to my day, one that's flexible enough to change if, or when, events pop up that are beyond my control. More importantly, it helps me to lay claim on the day. Time goes from something that's slipping between my fingers to a resource I'm using to my own ends.

When we fail to allocate a resource, it can all too quickly end up becoming frittered away.

It's all too easy, when we haven't structured our time, for our most pressing tasks to fall down our list of priorities, for the tyranny of the email inbox to have too much of a say in how our day should go, or for our labor to be repurposed by a colleague who wants to offload their own workload.

This approach is also useful in structuring your week overall, particularly as you develop your passion. Sitting down on a Sunday night, before the working week gets under way, and mapping out your time commitments, as well as how you can fit in the non-work tasks that simply have to get done, becomes a soothing ritual that mentally prepares you for the week ahead. If you're going to be careful how you allocate time to work duties, it's critically important that you treat your own, personal goals with the same care. You may even find that other people begin to respect your time more as well.

If your passion is writing, and your goal is to get published, ring-fence two or three periods during the week when you can lock yourself away and write. If your passion is art, and your goal is to master oil painting, then sign up to an evening class and commit to spending another one or two hours during the week practicing. If the thing you feel most passionate about is changing your job, allocate two or three one-hour periods of personal time during the week to pursuing the online course, or cultivating a network of contacts, that will help you achieve this goal.

It can feel counterintuitive to take the time we spend away from work and carve it up like this. Surely the point of having personal time is that it's unstructured and allows us to decompress after the working day? But time is a precious resource; if your employer is willing to pay you for the time you spend working on their projects, pay the same courtesy to your own goals, and give your projects the time they deserve.

We can often feel that time is the enemy: It either slips past us, taking with it our best intentions for the day, or else it drags, making meetings feel endless. But if you respect time, if you work with it instead of against it, you can begin to see big gains. It's true that schedules will occasionally slip, but by allocating time wisely you'll reap the rewards of meeting your objectives and knowing that you're working toward your goals.

THE POWER OF 'NO'

How often have you seen colleagues get bogged down in chores that have little to do with their core tasks, and that chip away at the time they can devote to their 'proper' job? How often have you seen a colleague being 'volunteered' for an 'exciting new challenge' that nobody else wants to undertake? How often have you left a colleague immersed in paperwork that somebody else failed to complete? How often have you been that colleague?

It's easy to fall into the trap of saying 'Yes' to too much. As human beings we like to feel needed. It gives our daily lives meaning to know that we helped out in some way, that we made a difference. It even forms the cornerstone of advice we give to young people who are starting out in their careers:

If you get a foot in the door, make yourself useful, make it difficult for your manager to imagine life there without you. But there's a considerable difference between volunteering for a project where you'll develop new skills and being the person lumbered with the thankless task of organizing the office Christmas party, year after year.

Too often, these extra tasks end up being clutter in our work schedules. They're the unwanted gifts that do nothing to help us progress toward our own goals and simply divert our time away from our own work and projects.

You may feel that you're building up brownie points with your manager, but ask yourself how valuable those brownie points actually are to you?

Any casualty of a redundancy scheme will tell you that when the corporate ax fell, any deposits they lodged in the bank of goodwill quickly became worthless.

The truth is, when you agree to other people's requests, you may well be saying 'No' to your own needs. No to focusing on your own tasks; no to developing new, more relevant skills; no to being open to opportunities that may lead to more exciting challenges in the future. Just as bringing minimalism into your home frees up energy that was tied up in clutter, applying the principles of minimalism in work – that is, focusing on the essential and removing all excess – will see you regain focus.

Have confidence in your own worth and in the talent and ability you bring to your own role. Many people feel wary about refusing to agree to requests at work: They feel it marks them out as 'not a team player' or 'unwilling to go the extra yard.' But if you already work hard at your core job role, then you're already a team player; you already go the extra yard. And if you work hard, you already have a long list of duties to be completed every day.

Saying no sets boundaries for the people around you. We tend to think of boundaries in negative terms, as things that limit our progress, hem us in. But boundaries define relationships and foster respect between people. Consider the manner in which 'good fences make good neighbors.' Such fences lend clarity to a situation, making it clear where everybody stands. It's this sense of clarity that leads to mutual respect, and is the basis of all good working relationships.

Saying 'No' need not sound confrontational.

Of course, a clear, simple 'No' is one option. But if you find this two-letter word difficult to utter, why not try another tack?

Firmly saying, 'I'd like to but I'm swamped with work!' gets the message across.

It's important that you feel comfortable turning down requests. (If nothing else, the person making the request may sense that you're not committed to your initial response, and persist in asking until you say yes!) So remember that you're not saying no to the person; these two letters don't reflect your relationship with them. You're saying no to the erosion of your quality of life. (If the request has come from a colleague to whom you're personally close, perhaps say this to them if it makes you feel more comfortable.)

You should also focus on the trade-off: Remind yourself that you're saying no so that you can concentrate on doing an excellent job of your existing tasks; so that you'll be fresh for tomorrow's presentation; so that you'll be able to give 100 percent. If it's relevant, remind yourself that the person making the request has his or her choice of people to ask, and there's a good chance they'll find somebody else to take on the task.

Remember, you're the only person
who can live your life.

Accept that saying no may make us unpopular in the moment – but saying a clear, graceful 'No' at an early stage can be the greatest gift you give your manager.

Very often, saying no is also about being kind to your future self. When I was younger, it was very easy to agree to work late on a project. I was single, and the stakes weren't particularly high – I wasn't obliged to pick up a child from kindergarten, or get home to care for an elderly relative. However, in agreeing, I always failed to remember the sensation I'd feel of fuming silently in a quiet office after hours, knowing that I'd volunteered to work this unpaid overtime. Part of growing up is knowing yourself and avoiding situations where you'll feel angry, or where you believe you've been the victim of manipulation. In life, there are all too many occasions where we have no control over our conditions – if you have the opportunity to opt out of feeling frustrated with yourself, take it.

It's essential to decide early on what your redline issues will be. Is your redline 'I will not work past 7 p.m.'? Then make this clear to your colleagues from the outset. Is your redline 'I won't accept work-related telephone calls at the weekend?' Then let everybody in your department know this, even if it's just in a conversational tone with your peers.

> Ultimately, saying no is about both
> setting boundaries and providing
> feedback to management.

After all, if you're being asked to take on extra duties on an ongoing basis, then either your organization is short-staffed or some of your colleagues are failing to pull their weight. If you're being lumbered with extra duties, week in, week out, then your role within the company has changed and your management team should recognize your enhanced responsibilities.

It's true that, in certain working environments, adopting such a stance may mean taking a huge gamble. But even if saying a direct, flat 'No' feels too daunting, try to harness that emotion by opening up a dialogue with your manager about your role, asking questions about the shifting of responsibilities within your workplace. You'll at least feel better for raising the issue, and you'll hopefully have laid down a marker to your boss that you're not an interchangeable cog in the office machine. In the end, however, if you feel that your employer is simply failing to appreciate your skills and abilities, perhaps it's time to start thinking about your long-term future with the company.

Tasks, bosses, even jobs all come and go. In the end, your greatest commitment is to yourself, and your most meaningful project should be that of giving yourself a fulfilling future.

QUALITY OVER QUANTITY

It was management consultant Peter Drucker who first said, 'There is nothing so useless as doing efficiently something that should not have been done at all.' I could have done with those words of wisdom when, in a job I had in recent years, I devised a system of color-coded rotas: the red files in my computer folder were at the draft stage, the orange ones were awaiting further information, and the green files were ready to be circulated to my colleagues. Over time, the system became more elaborate. There was a purple shade for rotas that had been confirmed but needed tinkering due to a request by a staffer, there was a tangerine shade for a rota that needed to be changed following a request by management.... Within a few weeks I was looking at a computer monitor that had more colors than the rainbow – but with little idea of what it all meant. What did a pink-colored folder signify again? Or one in sky blue? In the end, I had to go back to my former system of logging rotas in an old-fashioned notebook. It wasn't as snazzy as my color-coded system but it did the trick. Looking back, I was guilty of over-engineering a solution to a problem that didn't exist, and I should have directed some of that creative energy into streamlining other, more essential, areas of the role.

I was also guilty of engaging in performative 'busyness.' My actions screamed of somebody obsessed with 'being busy,' even if the net result was neither a better product nor an overall improvement in efficiency. Immersing ourselves in tasks that do little more than tinker around the edges of our core role, or that try to reinvent the wheel, are all ways in which we can find ourselves getting away from the essence of our role.

For decades, management consultants have spoken about the Pareto Principle, the observation that 80 percent of sales come from 20 percent of customers (it was management consultant Joseph M. Juran who first applied the work of Italian economist Vilfredo Pareto to business in the 1940s). When applied to productivity, it holds that just 20 percent of our efforts result in 80 percent of the results we get. The lesson is clear: Get busy – but get busy doing the activities that will result in the greatest possible outcome.

THE TRADE-OFF

Shonda Rhimes is one of the most successful people working in American television today. The creator of hit shows such as *Grey's Anatomy* and *Scandal*, she's said to be worth $135 million. So it was hardly a surprise when her Ivy League alma mater Dartmouth College asked the executive producer to give the commencement speech to the graduating class of 2014.

If the university authorities expected a few platitudes about the merits of her sterling education, they were wrong.

Instead, Ms Rhimes came clean about the struggles she faces as a single, working mother of three children. To those who regularly ask, 'Shonda, how do you do it all?' she has this reply: 'Whenever you see me succeeding in one area of my life, that almost certainly means I am failing in another. That is the trade-off. Anyone who tells you they are doing it all perfectly is a liar!'[24]

Ms Rhimes isn't alone, and while her experience illustrates the experience of working mothers, it also throws light on an uncomfortable truth that's relevant to everybody in the field of work: You simply can't excel at absolutely everything. It's unreasonable to expect anybody to be able to acquit themselves with excellence in every area of their lives. We don't expect a high school teacher to have the knowledge and skills to teach every school subject to the level required of an 18-year-old about to embark on a university education. Through their own innate skill and drive, they're skilled in two or three subjects at most, perhaps more if the subjects are closely related. If we can accept that specialization is part and parcel of a wide range of jobs, why can't we accept that specialization, along with focus, is the mark of all truly successful professionals?

Applying some of the principles of minimalism
can give you the mental space to decide what
aspects of your work you should focus on.

Yes, there will be trade-offs along the way – perhaps trade-offs
that you'll be uncomfortable with – but it's better to get three
or four tasks completed to perfection than produce nine or
10 tasks in a shoddy state. Trying to cover all the bases often
means that some crucial aspect of your job is going to suffer.
In stretching yourself too thin, very often all you're doing is
leaving yourself distressed by how your competence seems
to be failing you. But your competence isn't failing you – too
many demands are being placed on you.

The key is to accept that there will be trade-offs to be made.
What will simplify the process is the knowledge that there
will be points at which you'll have to make a call on what
to focus on. You'll need to ask yourself: *What is absolutely
essential? What will get me further along my journey toward
my destination?* So be armed with all of the facts and be ready
to decide which course of action is most important, which
tasks you must focus on, and when the time comes to make
a trade-off, be in a position where you can confidently take
ownership of your decision.

SMOOTH YOUR OWN PATH

Most of us assume that successful people are logistical geniuses who are tremendously good at organizing their time so that they can fit everything in. But truly effective people realize that it isn't possible to do it all, and structure their actions and their working lives to take cognizance of that. It can mean fighting our innate impulse to try to accommodate everybody, but it's an approach that chimes with our experience of watching successful people at work in their everyday lives.

One of the best managers I ever worked for simply refused to major in the minor stuff. With decades of experience at the top of his field, by the time I worked for him, Bill was preparing for retirement by working just two days a week at our office, a regional arm of the large company we worked for. We knew from the reverence with which the executive corps spoke about him that he was one of the best in the business, and there was always a sense of anticipation in knowing that he was flying in for a couple of days. It helped that he was an extremely hard worker – and very good company. But it was a friend of mine who noticed the extent to which Bill stuck to the task at hand, refusing to entertain any distractions that originated from outside our department. If his computer suffered a slowdown, he'd summon the on-call IT guy to his desk straight away – there was none of this nonsense of being instructed over the phone and being told 'Get back to me if it doesn't work after a restart....' Bill took the view that he was there to do a job, and it was the responsibility of his employers to make his experience as smooth as possible. If anything stood in the way of his doing that job, it had to be remedied. Updates on a computer system? That was IT's job, not his. Getting him from the airport on the other side of the city to our office? That was the office administrator's job. But getting the job done on time? Well, that was his job, and Bill was delighted to do it.

Bill set a good example of somebody who was able to focus on their own duties, who refused to get distracted by the non-essential issues that crop up in our work lives. It wasn't that he wasn't a team player – if the chips were down in the core part of his job, he'd pitch in and help – but if a problem emerged in an aspect of work that he wasn't qualified to deal with, say, the computer system, he had no hesitation in demanding prompt service to resolve the issue. He knew that other people had the expertise, and were employed to cover those tasks.

As we watched Bill sweep into the office for another busy day's work, dealing efficiently with the day's tasks and refusing to countenance hold-ups, my friend observed, 'Just look at Bill – it's like he's on casters....' It was an image that perfectly captured the frictionless nature of Bill's working conditions. He had structures in place that meant he could focus on the job in hand, and concentrate on managing a team.

Not everybody can call on the resources of a vast corporation to make their working life easier, but Bill illustrated the extent to which effective work calls for friction to be minimized.

The fewer distractions we encounter,
the easier it is to get work done.

The fewer speed bumps we meet along the way, the smoother our progress toward our goal. The retail industry has understood this for years: You no longer have to go through the ordeal of leaving your home and traveling to a shop to buy a new outfit; all you have to do is press a button on your smartphone and your dress will arrive at your door within a few days.

You can take the same approach by removing as much friction as possible from your working life. Minimalism helps with this by removing physical clutter from your surroundings, so bring some of that philosophy into the office and streamline your immediate surroundings and your processes. After all, extraneous clutter in your working environment just becomes a series of decisions that have to be made, and even a decision as meaningless as 'Which of my seven pens will I use today?' uses mental energy that would be better devoted to getting your job done. Instead of constantly checking your email and letting the latest missive from marketing disrupt the order of your to-do list, commit to checking in with your account only at certain times of the day, and being strict with which emails you choose to act upon and which emails you delete.

THE FUNDAMENTALS

Earlier we asked the question: what is absolutely essential? What will get you closer to your destination? Obviously, that applies to individual tasks within your role, but it's also a question that has to be regularly asked about the job itself. How does it get you closer to your ultimate goal? Your role may have served you well when you were a young graduate, or when you were returning to the paid workforce after years spent caring for your children, or when your financial outgoings were less onerous. But how does your current job – with its current obligations, and its current opportunities – sit with what you want to do with your life?

It's common to outgrow a role. Every time we start a new job, we face a fresh learning curve, and in mastering new terrains we grow from the experience. But after a while, we sometimes can realize that we're stagnating; we're no longer challenged, or our role has changed so much over the years that it's no longer recognizable, or our own interests and priorities have changed. In short, our role may no longer be meeting our needs, and is failing to resonate with our values and goals in life.

If there's too much in your job that fails to serve the purpose of furthering your personal goals, this is a distraction that must be eliminated. Obviously, leaving a job isn't always a practical option, but if you don't have the impetus to consciously decide where you want to go, your energy will either dissipate into projects that do nothing for your goals, or be subsumed and used to fuel somebody else's ambition.

Deciding to leave an organization can be a wrench. In a culture where the first question we're asked at parties is, 'What do you do?,' our choice of profession often makes up a large part of our identity, and the thought of our status changing is bound to induce a certain amount of anxiety. But if the role is failing you, what are you gaining from it?

Brenda had worked in the same job for years – though in many ways she'd worked in it only nominally as her duties became both more stressful and boring. She'd mastered the core tasks easily in the early days, but successive rounds of restructuring within the firm had seen her pressed into taking on more and more duties over the years. Friends told her to apply for other jobs within the industry; that with her experience she was bound to get something else. But although Brenda paid lip service to her friends' suggestions, she dragged her heels and her CV remained years out of date. She may not have been particularly happy, but she had the measure of the job. Plus, she felt all of the hard work she'd put in over the years was about to pay off. She just knew it.

In the end, the decision was taken out of her hands when she lost her job in a round of involuntary redundancies.

Brenda's mistake was to fail to heed her misgivings about her role due to a common error: sunk cost bias. Sunk cost bias is a widely recognized psychological phenomenon that occurs when we factor in the time, effort, or money we've already expended on a project and feel that we can't walk away because we've made an 'investment.' Brenda felt that she was on track for promotion; that her years of working late and taking on extra responsibilities were about to pay off. She felt that if she were to leave, she'd be walking away from her 'investment.' In the event, her 'investment' never paid off.

Brenda got a sharp lesson in the realities of corporate life when she received her severance payment. Many others also spend years waiting for their investment of time or effort to pay off, and grow increasingly frustrated waiting for the day that their loyalty will be recognized and they'll finally be ushered into the job they feel they deserve.

THE COMFORT ZONE

Meanwhile, too many of us stick with the routine of familiar circumstances, even if it's a bit annoying or gradually grinding us down, merely because we've become experts in handling them.

It's worth regularly checking in with yourself and posing the question: 'Is this the situation that I really want?

And if I'm not happy, is there an end in sight?' Are you holding out for a dream job that's realistically within your grasp? Be honest with yourself. Even better, sit down with your boss and set out the future you see for yourself. If your dream job is your boss's own role, deploy some tact and say that you'd be willing to take on some of their responsibilities – responsibilities that will further your own ambitions. How does that chime with their view of your role – and, more specifically, your role going into the future?

An essential step in achieving our goals is giving voice to them, and sharing them with the individuals who can help bring them on. Most bosses are interested in motivating their staff to fulfill their potential and to contribute to the organization at the optimum level, so it would be within their interest to keep you on track. If you get a sense that your boss doesn't take your ambitions seriously, or if the company simply doesn't foster a culture of discussing with staff which of their talents to utilize, then it's definitely time to quietly update your CV and refresh your LinkedIn profile.

BE MORE THAN YOUR JOB

Sometimes, our greatest obstacle to radical growth is ourselves, or our image of ourselves. Think about how often you introduce yourself to somebody at a party by describing how you earn a living: 'I'm Mary and I'm a teacher....' 'I'm John and I'm an accountant....' These job descriptions do a lot of the heavy lifting in communicating information about ourselves to strangers, so they're useful, but they can also be a constraining influence – surely you're much more than what you do for eight hours a day?

We may feel that our jobs give us our identity, so leaving a job can feel like a powerful undoing of oneself.

But if minimalism teaches us anything, it's that each of us is more than the possessions we own or whichever identity we slip on when we leave home in the morning. And sometimes identities that are based on our job or career do little more than hold us back from progressing toward true fulfillment. As one of novelist Toni Morrison's characters memorably said, 'You wanna fly, you gotta give up the shit that weighs you down.'[25]

Ultimately, just like your possessions, your work life should work for you – and you shouldn't live for work. You may already be lucky enough to have a job that you find fulfilling and which feeds your soul, but everybody has the scope to improve their lives, either through finding a role that's in line with their passion or by creating the opportunities that will give them the psychological space to pursue their personal goals.

Most of us expect to spend at least four decades of our lives in the world of work. Given the vast amounts of time we spend there, it's essential that work provides us not just with our daily bread, but with a sense of purpose.

So, define your work goal by looking to the values that you hold dear and the life that you want for yourself. Now break things down and determine the steps required to reach your goal. Do you need to upskill? Do you need to gain experience in different departments? Do you need to develop a network of contacts in the field you'd like to move into? You might argue that each of these actions call for considerable commitments of time and energy, and you'd be right. The fact is that real change can only come about by you setting a course for your goal and taking the actions that will achieve it, even if it means letting other, lesser tasks fall by the wayside.

Always ask: what brings value to my life? What will serve to get me closer to my ultimate goal? Sometimes this will apply to certain tasks you meet along the way. However, sometimes this will apply to your whole job.

Decide how to use your talents purposefully. What we focus on and engage in has a habit of assuming a greater and greater role in our lives, so be deliberate about where you expend your energy.

CHAPTER 3

WAKE UP YOUR WALLET

If the purpose of minimalism is to get rid of excess clutter and bring intentionality into your life, doesn't it make sense that the same sense of being deliberate and purposeful would extend to one of the most limited of your resources: your money?

It seems laughable now, but when I was a little girl, my friends and I were fixated on 1980s TV soaps like *Dallas* and *Dynasty*. The minutiae of the high-octane business deals went over our heads, but one thing we could understand was that successful women, like Linda Gray's Sue Ellen Ewing and Joan Collins's Alexis Carrington, had to have impeccable taste in men and designer clothes.

Roll on a decade or so, and although the extravagant bejeweled shoulder pads had given way to the smart pantsuit, I still labored under the impression that in order to look the part of a young professional I had to have a vast wardrobe of 'looks.' It was the 1990s, and I'd watched enough sitcoms to know that it was my duty as a twentysomething woman to have a roster of cute outfits and a large collection of shoes at my disposal. I had no real sense of style, but I was an enthusiastic consumer of magazines, and the pile-em-high ethos of the budget chain stores I shopped at meant that individual purchases didn't carry particularly high stakes. Did I really want that pair of brown jacquard-print pants? Who cared? They were cheap, and I was bound to get at least some wear out of them. As my payday purchases mounted up, I failed to notice that my female colleagues, those more established in their fields, weren't gripped by the same mania to stay abreast of fashion. Despite this, they still managed to look stylish and well put-together. My boss was a rangy New Zealander whose duties regularly took her to the rugby sidelines, so her day-to-day look was practical with a hint of adventure. Meanwhile, one of our other colleagues did an impressive line in tailored pants and ankle boots that flattered her slim figure.

Looking back, I cringe both at how much I spent and how desperate I was to shoehorn myself into my new role of 'young working woman.' I was buying into the perception that in order to dress for success, I had to acquire a new item of clothing every week, and at least give the impression that I was spending a fortune in shops and boutiques.

All these years later, I have a more practical approach to my wardrobe. When I go shopping, my main concerns are less, 'Is this stylish?' and more 'Does this fit?' Does this fit my middle-aged figure – and does it fit my life?

Earlier we saw how easy it is for a little homeware purchase to become clutter in our home. That's because, before it becomes part of the hodgepodge of disused junk hidden away in the corner of the spare room, it arrives in the home without any thought being given to how it'll fit in there. I must admit, I've done it myself: when embarking on a declutter, I've discovered items that I've never used, perhaps in their original packaging or even the carrier bag I brought them home in. Just the other day, I found two gift vouchers tucked away inside a book I was about to send to the charity shop. The accompanying receipt showed they had been purchased in December 2013, on one of those frantic shopping days leading up to the holiday season. It all came back to me: I'd bought them as gifts for two family members, and then mislaid them. The fact that I must have gone out and bought replacement presents even closer to Christmas Day only irked me even more. The reality of the situation was that holiday-season mania had me in its grip, and any good habits I've built up over the years completely deserted me in those hectic days.

That reckless attitude to my own hard-earned cash, where I could spend it so blithely and with such little care that I could misplace two valuable pieces of plastic, goes to the heart of why I need minimalism in my life: to counteract those occasional impulses to engage in mindless spending.

> We all spend more than we should on
> items we don't strictly need.

British women spend on average £1,042 on clothes every year, yet end up wearing just 55 percent of what's in their wardrobe. Meanwhile, it's estimated that British people have £10 billion worth of clothes stashed away in their wardrobes, largely unworn.[26]

But more and more people have begun asking questions about their own spending choices, and how their decisions over their money have consequences for themselves and for the world at large.

THE REAL COST OF BUYING CHEAP

Just a few decades ago – probably around the time that I was following glossy TV soap operas – new clothes were an occasional purchase, an investment to be weighed up carefully because the garment would likely spend a few years in one's wardrobe before finally being passed on to a friend, younger sibling, or charity. But from the 1990s, the combination of cheap credit and the development of a globalized manufacturing economy meant countries in the developed world were suddenly able to avail themselves of cheap consumer goods on a level never previously seen.

Within just a few years, the phenomenon as it applied to clothing had been dubbed 'fast fashion' – tops, dresses, and shoes that were designed to be worn a handful of times before being disposed of – and had gained a foothold in the market. And as the business model spread across other consumer goods, prices were driven downward, and items from sweaters to MP3 players became much more frequent purchases.

For instance, I remember the thrill of buying a personal stereo in the 1980s. I was 12 years old, and the Sony Walkman represented the height of technological advance. In order to afford the simple tape deck and flimsy foam headphones, I had to save up my weekly allowance and carefully guard every extra cent that came my way over a period of months, during which time I'd attentively monitor the price of competitor devices in the electronics shop in my nearest big town. When the great day finally arrived, it was with a considerable sense of achievement that I handed over the princely sum of £36 (about $50) for my new personal stereo.

In the decades since then, I must have spent thousands on electronic equipment – on television sets, MP3 players, computers, smartphones – but I don't think I've ever been as delighted with a single purchase as I was with that Walkman on that day in 1987. Of course, I couldn't have known then that in the years to follow, the developed world would be subsumed by a tidal wave of cheap consumer goods; nor could I have known the effect they would have on the Earth due to the pillaging of its resources for their production.

Today, more and more people find that spending $10 on a shirt that was manufactured for mere cents in the developing world sits uneasily with them. This kind of price raises questions about levels of pay for the workers who made the shirt, and the burden placed on those workers – who may have been exposed to hazardous chemicals or obliged to work in unregulated conditions.

Meanwhile, according to Greenpeace International, the move toward fast fashion means we're consuming and dumping fashion at a higher rate than the planet can handle.[27] Thousands of tons of synthetic fibers enter British waters every year,[28] while polyester is responsible for the release of nearly three times as much carbon over its life cycle than cotton is.[29]

By late 2019, at least some quarters of the fashion industry could identify the mechanism at play. 'The rise of fast fashion has distorted our relationship with fashion and design,' designer Stella McCartney said in an open letter to her counterparts in the industry as she launched a range that emphasized sustainability. 'In the current system, designers set trends, fast-fashion copies these trends and force-feeds them to us.'[30]

In buying armfuls of generically manufactured
T-shirts from the developing world, we may
be turning our backs on skilled designers
and talented creators closer to home.

These young entrepreneurs also work hard and would equally appreciate the financial backing of a few paying customers. Those splurges – either at the tills of our local budget chain store on payday or on online portals late at night – serve to fill our wardrobes with cheap clothes, line the pockets of vast retail giants, and little else.

Imagine if the money spent on snapping up five versions of the same sweater instead went toward a wardrobe staple created by somebody in your own city. Somebody whose designs you discovered at a local market, or who took the time to pen a handwritten note before slipping the order to you in the mail. And imagine if designers in the developing world were able to find a burgeoning local market for their work, instead of facing a market saturated with second-hand clothes shipped in from the developed world.

If minimalism is about bringing intentionality into one's life, the choices we make as consumers could make an obvious place to lay down a marker. In this book's introduction, we looked at how we can stem the flow of goods coming into our homes, to make room for a better life for ourselves. However, we're required to engage with consumer culture on an almost daily basis, so even if we're already conscientious about what we bring into our homes, it's worth thinking about where we direct our purchasing power when we use it.

As we've seen, minimalism isn't about penny-pinching. It's about bringing intentionality into our life. By making informed decisions about where and how we spend our money, we direct our focus outward, helping, hopefully, to create a better world by virtue of our choices.

FOR THE LOVE OF MONEY

At some stage, we've all been told that money can't buy us happiness. As it turns out, science backs that up. It's almost a decade since Nobel Prize-winning psychologist Daniel Kahneman published a study into salary and satisfaction with one's life. The study found that while happiness increases as salary goes up, it levels off at about $75,000. At the time of the study, Kahneman speculated that $75,000 represented 'a threshold beyond which further increases in income no longer improve individuals' ability to do what matters most to their emotional well-being, such as spending time with people they like, avoiding pain and disease, and enjoying leisure.'[31]

> While earning more money will make you happier, beyond a certain point more money won't make you significantly more content.

Meanwhile, studies in the 1970s identified a phenomenon that had been noted by philosophers for hundreds of years. Psychologists termed it the hedonic adaptation effect, or the mind's powerful ability to adjust to new circumstances, and reset what it'll take to make us happy.

A 1978 study by psychologists Brickman, Coates, and Janoff-Bulman looked at overall levels of happiness in lottery winners and people who'd been left in a paraplegic state following injury. The study evaluated the subjects' outlooks in the early days of either winning a substantial cash prize or being told that they were now in a paraplegic state, with researchers returning some months later to measure their outlooks once more. As you'd expect, in the wake of these life-changing events, the lottery winners were upbeat and positive, while those in a paraplegic state were more somber and negative when interviewed. Remarkably, when researchers interviewed them some time later, both groups' happiness levels were close to those found in the general population. In other words, they weren't appreciably happier or unhappier than before, even though their life circumstances were radically altered.[32]

Just think about that for a second: the lottery winner who never has to worry about money ever again, and who can set off on a world cruise at the drop of a hat, feels roughly the same as he did on the day before his winning numbers came up. The implications of this research are that our circumstances may change, but our overall outlook and attitude toward life end up returning to where they've always been.

We tend to be unaware of this when we volunteer for a little life upgrade; when, say, we award ourselves with a little treat after a pay rise.

After the initial thrill of hearing that our hard work is about to be recognized, we often start planning how we'll use the extra money.

This might be an upgrade to our mobile phone package; a new, more luxurious moisturizer; or a subscription to a recipe box delivery service. On the face of it, these are all measures that would enhance our lives – a new smartphone, well-hydrated skin, less time spent cooking – but within a few months, our satisfaction levels will have returned to where they were before we got our pay rise.

Except that now, we're locked into a new mobile phone contract, we're afraid to stop using the expensive, high-quality moisturizer in case we shrivel up, and we've made other commitments instead of spending time shopping for food. All we have to show for the pay rise that left us so thrilled just months ago is a slightly bigger figure on our pay slip. The material gain to us has been lost.

Minimalism offers us useful tools for fighting this phenomenon, which is known as the hedonic treadmill. Being mindful of the limitations of what money can achieve makes us aware that these little boosts in our material circumstances don't have a lasting effect on our emotional well-being. Ultimately, money – and the goods and services it can buy – is supposed to serve us. And if the outcome is no net gain, then why indulge?

Of course, as with every other area of life, this is a judgment call that only you can make, based on your own circumstances. For instance, after owning a car for a number of years, I decided to get rid of it. I live in a city, and I can make my way around by bike or public transportation. When I had a car, it mostly stayed in its parking space, downstairs from my apartment. And every now and again, I'd find myself thinking, *That car. It's just sitting there, doing nothing, while I'm paying tax and insurance on it...* before taking it to work simply to justify its presence in my life. I wish I could say that I had a road to

Damascus moment that ended my relationship with that Ford Focus. Instead, in the end, it was a sky-high repair bill that put paid to my status as a car owner. Nowadays, I no longer have to cover the cost of insurance or auto tax, and if I 'need' a car (if I want to pick up a friend from across town, shop for bulky grocery items, or visit relations in a different part of the country), I either avail myself of a local car-sharing service or hire a car from a rental company.

On the other hand, if you have young children who must be taken to childcare every day, you live in the countryside, or you have an elderly relative who depends on you for transport to doctor's appointments or to attend worship on Sundays, owning a car may be unavoidable.

Minimalism isn't about living your
life along hard and fast rules.

It's about thinking carefully about the issues you face, and coming up with a solution that works for you and your family. It's about discerning your own genuine needs as opposed to supposed 'needs' for material goods that consumerism tries to impose on us all, or buying into a lifestyle that may not serve you well in the long term.

In the end, minimalists excel at weighing up all the options, making conscious decisions about their lifestyle, and set a course for the life they want for themselves and their family, not the life that capitalism has set out for them.

TO SPEND OR NOT TO SPEND

The American money guru Dave Ramsey wryly summed up the situation so many of us find ourselves in: 'We buy things we don't need with money we don't have... to impress people we don't like.'[33]

It would be funny if it weren't so devastatingly close to the bone. So many of the purchases we make aren't simply for the purpose of fulfilling a need or even providing us with the momentary feeling of happiness identified in the previous pages. In our own lives, we've all seen instances of people buying expensive consumer goods as status symbols, using them as items that will telegraph their material success to the world at large. The couples who buy a high-spec, rugged Land Rover even though they never leave the paved roads of suburbia, the executive who buys designer labels simply because of the clothes' association with a big-name celebrity, the young homeowner who buys the glass coffee maker she saw an Instagram star use.

All of us like to believe we're part of a tribe, that we belong to a community of like-minded individuals. When so many of us have grown up in a consumer culture, it's tempting to think that we can buy our way into our tribe, or secure our position in it, by surrounding ourselves with the right gear.

Ask yourself: *Am I trying to gain entry to a certain lifestyle or a peer group by purchasing the 'right' smartphone, by signing up to the 'right' beauty-box subscription service? Is membership of this smart set worth the financial outlay involved? Will spending cash in this way help me progress toward my own personal goals?*

Sometimes our decision to make a purchase is simply feeding a need we experience in the heat of the moment.

Experts in self-care have long recognized the potential for confusing one state for another, and the danger of trying to 'fix' things by feeding a pseudo-desire instead of addressing the real issue. In social counseling, practitioners use the acronym HALT as a reminder that people are particularly vulnerable to poor decision-making when they're hungry, angry, lonely, or tired. And in our quieter moments, it's easy to identify those instances in our past when our judgment in relation to something as supposedly rational as our consumer choices was clouded by emotions that had nothing to do with the job in hand.

None of this is to belittle anybody who actively chooses to invest in items that bring them joy, such as designer clothes. For some people, clothes are a powerful form of self-expression. Their carefully curated wardrobe choices form a vital creative outlet in a stressful or uninspiring nine-to-five work life and have always formed a part of their identity, going all the way back to the days when, as students, they used to rifle through charity shops for bargains. If this sounds like you, then clothes, and the self-expression they afford you, are clearly connected to one of your core values.

However, for many of us, shopping for clothes is a broadly idle pursuit that we engage in on a rather mindless basis. We may do it because we're bored, or we're stressed, or because we're hungry, angry, lonely, or tired. Or we may do it simply because we're rather shy young women trying to buy good taste. Instead of shelling out for a new leather jacket that you'll hardly ever wear, try addressing whatever issue is underlying this need.

MATERIAL WORLD

As much as society cheers us on in the pursuit of material goods that will signal our success, materialism appears to do us few favors. Research shows that materialism fosters isolation, and the pursuit of consumer goods for their own sake leads to lower emotional well-being.[34] As psychology professor Tim Kasser reported following his research into the subject: 'The more highly people endorsed materialistic values, the more they experienced unpleasant emotions, depression and anxiety, the more they reported physical health problems, such as stomach aches and headaches, and the less they experienced pleasant emotions and felt satisfied with their lives.'[35]

It's possible to feel abundant with less.

If you've already made progress in decluttering your home, you'll by now be familiar with the luxurious feeling of being surrounded by more space. What was a cramped living room is now airy and feels bigger somehow. The items you've decided to hang on to have a value that's personal to you – they either perform a function in your life or they mean something to you. Even better, they're not subsumed under a tide of stuff that means nothing to you.

Now that your living room has been cleared of debris, you can appreciate the finely crafted workmanship that went into making the sideboard you inherited from your grandmother. Now that opening your wardrobe doesn't occasion a deluge of never-worn, cheap tank tops, you can savor the merino sweater you were keeping for good wear. Now that the various moisturizers and skin cleansers that used to litter your bathroom shelf have been dumped, your bathroom is once more an oasis of calm, a sanctuary that's almost worthy of a show house.

In a way, deriving joy from the possessions we already have underpins a theory of true materialism promoted by sociologist and economist Juliet Schor. Her form of materialism is characterized not by an excessive desire for more goods but an appreciation for the material qualities of an object. She argues that by being fully aware of the labor and resources that went into making and transporting a product, we can cherish its role in our life for that little bit longer, or at least beyond the point at which consumer culture deems it to be out of fashion.[36]

SAVE YOUR PENNIES

What appeals to practitioners of minimalism is the manner in which decluttering encourages simplicity in one's life. Consider the items you've curated to fit in with your life. What more do you need?

For increasing numbers of people, the answer is: financial freedom, rather than material goods. Members of the Financial Independence, Retire Early (FIRE) movement have embraced this approach. It's an intoxicating proposition: instead of spending your thirties, forties, and fifties in the service of an employer, all in the hope of finally earning your freedom in your sixties, why not live the life of a financially independent person while you're still young enough to enjoy the benefits? Right at the heart of how FIRE works, however, is saving heavily (and investing the savings), avoiding consumer debt, and paring down other forms of debt (student loans, home mortgages) by making certain critical lifestyle choices. FIRE takes the view that driving expensive cars, buying large houses, and filling one's life with status symbols only slows down your progress toward the goal of financial independence. The reward, they say, is the freedom to walk away from your job – or reduce your hours, or take regular 'mini-retirements' – and pursue personal fulfillment while in your thirties or forties.

The FIRE movement may be a little too extreme for many of us, but for people who have been caught up in a cycle of upgrading their lifestyle every few years, it offers a fresh way of thinking, such as: *I could buy a new car now... or I could continue to drive my old runabout and direct the money I'd have used on a car loan toward my savings account. Now that I have a new job, I could buy an expensive new house... or I could simply stay in my small apartment and make larger payments off my mortgage. I could strip out our kitchen and install a version of the kitchen I saw on that home makeover show the other night... or I could top up my pension.*

SHARE AND SHARE ALIKE

Meanwhile, if life seems a little too simple, a little too pared down to be practical, technology and a fast-developing sharing economy is here to help. I mentioned earlier that I used a car-sharing service, which means that I can drive a car for a modest sum that's based on the amount of time that I use it for and the distance I drive. The same principle is being rolled out to a series of goods and services. After all, the average power drill is used for between nine and 17 minutes over its entire lifetime.[37] Now that tracking technology has made short-term leasing of equipment a practical proposition, an entire industry has developed around trying to make use of some of our possessions' downtime. Experts predict that the sharing economy will be worth $335 billion by 2025.[38]

The sharing economy offers many of the benefits
of ownership, without many of the responsibilities
of storing or maintaining equipment.

It also means not going into debt to accumulate the 'essential' markers of success. After all, for more and more people, success is defined not by the snazzy new car that you drive (particularly if it was purchased on the back of credit). Instead, success means living within one's means and focusing on what is actually important in life: relationships with the people we care about.

HOW WE LOST CONTROL OF OUR SPENDING

For many people, the economic mistakes made in the years before the Great Recession of 2008 can be traced back to the expansion of personal credit by the banking system, and the widespread consumerism that it facilitated. In the 1980s, 1990s, and 2000s, success became synonymous with high-spec cars that weren't suited to our needs, and vast mansions appointed with multiple living spaces and equipped with big rooms that begged to be filled with furniture, TVs, sound systems, and bric-a-brac. It's been well documented that for many families, this level of spending was beyond their means, with cheap credit often making up the shortfall between what people earned and the lifestyle they believed they were entitled to.

In hearts and minds, what fueled this 'because I'm worth it' culture was rampant consumerism.

It was a force by which people found fleeting self-expression and a form of fulfillment by purchasing consumer goods.

In the early part of the 20th century, this was underpinned by technological advances that made tangible and lasting differences to people's lives, including the refrigerator, the electric light, and the motorcar. But by the 1980s, slick marketeers had mastered the art of persuading people to yearn for items they didn't really need, and marketing professionals put their skills to considerable use.

Then mainstream culture rowed in to boost demand for consumer goods. TV programs and movies – from *Ferris Bueller's Day Off* to *Friends* – depicted middle-class figures whose lives were awash with the latest conveniences, who wore the latest fashions, and whose adventures and lifestyles weren't constrained in any way by economic concerns.

Meanwhile, newspapers and magazines embraced the editorial ease of 'lifestyle journalism,' which now devoted acres of newsprint to consumer trends and advances in fashion and interiors. (In the 1970s, one high-profile and prestigious newspaper, the *Financial Times*, started a single-page round-up of the latest consumer goods, called 'How To Spend It'; by 1994 it had grown to an entire pullout glossy magazine in the paper's Saturday edition.)

In addition, an activity as mundane as shopping was pitched to us as a pleasurable pastime, even a form of therapy. What had been for years an unavoidable and sometimes stressful use of our time was reframed as the ultimate form of relaxation.

While there's undoubtedly a sense of satisfaction in finding the perfect pair of shoes for an upcoming event, the way shopping – which is no more than the exchange of goods and services for our cash – has been presented in the media, as some sort of a reward to aspire to, has been a considerable feat of psychological engineering for the retail industry.

In too many respects, the attitude that redemption could be achieved by toting a credit card was one that leached into our culture at large.

It created a notion that people – mostly women, it has to be said – desired little more than a splurge at a boutique, like Julia Roberts' character in *Pretty Woman*. Really, it's little wonder that people who have come of age since the 1980s have navigated much of their adult life under the de facto doctrine that indulgence and even personal satisfaction can only be obtained by returning home with a half-dozen bags bursting at the seams with purchases.

But isn't this a little insulting? To imply that vastly complicated beings like ourselves, who have overcome obstacles and worked hard to get to where we are in life, would wish for nothing more than a slightly sophisticated version of *Supermarket Sweep*? That people whose hopes and dreams may range from gaining a professional qualification to starting a family to building a dream home, have as the pinnacle of their material desires the wish to give over a day to rummaging around in a cluttered outlet store.

SLEEP ON IT

My friend adores shopping. The bright lights, the muzak, the hustle and bustle of a department store – this is where she feels at home. And she's a champion shopper, relishing every purchase. Every completed purchase, that is. For as much as she enjoys eyeing up the latest fashions or appraising the merits of a new beauty product, she ends up taking very few products home with her:

I used to overspend. If I saw a new dress in a magazine, and I spotted it in town, I had to have it. But that was unsustainable. I still love checking out what's new on the rails, but I know that it's my love of something novel; I know that if I bring it home, there's a good chance that I'll be sick of it within a few weeks and it'll simply go to a charity shop.

So instead, I'll pick up the item that's caught my eye and inspect it thoroughly. I'm getting information about how it will wear, how it looks against my skin tone, how it fits…. I'm really getting a feel for it. And just on the point where I'm about to bring it to the checkout, I'll put it back. I'll go home and think about how I'd use it, and how often. And if I can still see its merits two days later, I'll return to the shop and buy it.

The two-day wait makes me weigh up whether I really want the dress – or pair of jeans, or whatever. And it feels twice as nice when I finally get it home, as the sense of anticipation has built up.

I'd tried Prue's approach myself, and it's transformative. I can pick up an item and appreciate the workmanship that went into it, the quality of the materials, and then return it to the shelf.

Very often, before I've even left the shop I'll have decided that I don't need or want the product.

Sometimes the greatest satisfaction is in simply holding an item and possessing it in the moment. But if afterward I believe it can bring genuine value to my life, I'll return two days later and pony up the cash.

It's a habit that probably wouldn't find favor with the retail and advertising industry, but ultimately no matter what the advertising industry would contend, the most satisfying form of personal fulfillment involves being purposeful with one's money… and having a healthy bank balance.

Strategies to shop smart

So, how can you fight the forces of advertising, social pressure, and simple greed as you negotiate the retail landscape? Here are a few tips:

1. Rethink your consumption of TV and social media

Until a few years ago, advertisers would pour billions of dollars into the coffers of television networks, desperate to get their commercial aired during a popular drama or sportscast. Television still has a strong grip on our culture, but social media is increasingly hoovering up advertising budgets as companies target its myriad users. The net result is a deluge of commercially driven messages tempting us to buy things we don't really need. But by reducing your exposure to television and social media, you'll reduce your exposure to such influences. Take advantage of the technological advances that mean you no longer have to watch the documentary about your favorite musician at the single time it's broadcast along with its attendant commercials. Thanks to streaming services and cable subscription packages, it's now possible to largely remove TV ads from your viewing experience, also allowing you to focus on the show. With social media, be selective in whose Twitter feeds and Instagram stories you follow, prioritizing trusted voices in the fields you're interested in, and avoiding the ream of vacuous tweets and promoted Instagram posts. In addition, impose a cap on the amount of time you spend watching TV or following social media. If you commit to spending no more than an hour watching television, say, it's less likely you'll find yourself watching garbage.

2. Assess whether there's a better use for your money

Proponents of the Financial Independence, Retire Early movement work and save hard in order to have greater choice over how they utilize their time in the years to come. Their accelerated saving schedules may not be appropriate for your lifestyle or circumstances, but their attitude throws light on the point that money can be banked and has the potential to be repurposed as free time at a later date. On that basis, would the $100 pair of stylish yoga pants you fancy be a worthwhile purchase? When you consider how long it took you to earn that sum, would buying those pants represent a good use of that time and labor? Or would it be better spent on a night out with friends, paying a little extra toward your pension, or in the savings account marked 'Galapagos'? Only you can decide how you'll spend your own money, but isn't it thinking beyond one's material desire?

3. Pay with cash to keep track of your spending

I'm old enough to remember when owning a credit card had a touch of glamor about it. Part of its appeal was that it appeared to have magic powers: according to a succession of TV ads that screened during my childhood, the mere production of a credit card from a wallet or purse would see hotel receptionists stand a little taller, restaurant waiters become more attentive, and shop assistants smile more warmly. It offered the promise of a life lived with little effort, and without the vulgar business of exchanging notes or coins. In recent years, this feature has extended to ATM cards tied to our current accounts and even to our smartphones. However, this frictionless spending can lead to money flowing out of our accounts without our even noticing. One way of tackling this mindless spending is by using cash for everyday purchases, making small and medium-size transactions feel more real. This means we have to set a budget as we anticipate how much money we'll need to cover our purchases, while the act of counting out notes and coins makes us aware that we are drawing on a finite resource.

4. Be an anthropologist

In opening Selfridges in 1909, Harry Gordon Selfridge introduced such innovations as placing stock on open display instead of storing the fashionable dresses and smart suits in wooden cabinets; pumping cinnamon fragrance onto the trading floor; and opening a restroom for women shoppers. He turned shopping into recreation, taking out newspaper adverts that compared a trip to the resplendent department store to 'sightseeing.'[39] In the 21st century, retailers continue to employ tactics to coax a few dollars from us, hoping to make shopping attractive with their sleek window displays, piped music or spacious fitting rooms. Retailers also realize that not everybody relishes trips to large stores, so they use social media to remind us that their vast stock inventory is available to us at the click of a button. Being aware of how retailers try to persuade us to spend our money can help us disentangle our impulses from our true desires. Do I really want this perfume, or am I falling under the spell of the persuasive assistant? Am I the kind of shopper being targeted by the music that's powering out of the sound system, and is this making me more susceptible to the store's tactics? When I shop, I like to think I'm summoning my inner 'retail anthropologist': by inspecting my surroundings I can take a step back from the situation and determine what I really need and what's just window dressing.

5. Make a list before you shop

I'll confess: I'm one of those people whose unreliable memory means that I rely on lists. I find that it focuses the mind as I enter an environment where retailers have invested huge sums in trying to persuade shoppers to part with their money. Here's another confession: I'm easily distracted, and I find that if I enter a shop with a vague intention to buy, say, something healthy for dinner, I'll leave with something healthy... and enough unhealthy snacks for three days. Drawing up an old-fashioned shopping list – or even compiling one on your smartphone – and referring back to it regularly keeps you on track in an environment that's designed to make you spend. It means you concentrate on the task in hand, rather than allowing your attention to wander to the bargains aisle.

6. Apply the two-day rule

The new cleanser that your favorite beauty influencer has been talking about has materialized before you in your local drugstore. It's a miracle! But it's twice as expensive as your regular make-up remover. What to do? Honestly? Put it back on the shelf, walk away, and hold off on buying it for at least 24 hours. If, after a night's sleep, you're still thinking about the cleanser, check out the reviews that have been posted online. Wait another 24 hours. Ask yourself: *Do I really need that new cleanser? How would it improve my life? Am I simply hankering after the thrill of something new?* If you're still convinced that you should buy it, go ahead. Thanks to modern inventory control practices, there's zero chance that the item will be sold out within two days. If you particularly desire the item, you'll find that a two-day wait for make-up remover, a new dress, or a new pair of trainers that you particularly want is perfectly manageable.

7. Borrow instead of buy

Before buying a new appliance or item of clothing, ask yourself if it's something you can borrow or rent instead. Thanks to the fast-growing sharing economy, there's great scope for hiring items which are used on only an occasional basis, from power drills to removal vans. Meanwhile, for women like me, for whom fashion is a foreign concept, dress hire shops provide the perfect solution when invitations to weddings come through the letterbox. They let me have the sensation of feeling stylish, without paying vast sums of money for the pleasure. Meanwhile, don't underestimate the untapped resources within your own social network. If you're considering buying a plush Kenwood food processor for a small kitchen project, why not first check with your friends to see if they have one? In many homes, food processors do little more than take up valuable kitchen real estate. You may find that your friend will gladly lend it to you for a period – and even more gladly accept a bottle of wine given in thanks.

8. Ask whether you have space for the item

We saw in Chapter 1 just how difficult it can be to accommodate the possessions you already have – your clothes, your gadgets, your books…. So before you bring home a bread-maker you found on sale, think long and hard about where it'll fit in your kitchen. Can you justify losing the valuable counter space it'll take up? Would it end up being squeezed into a kitchen cupboard then going unused because it's out of sight? Would it finally become just another item of clutter? If you don't see a long-term home for your potential new purchase, just make a call there and then, and simply let it stay in the department store.

9. Buy quality items

We're all familiar with the phrase: 'Buy cheap, buy twice,' and I know that I've regretted buying inexpensive shoes, for example, and discovering too late that they're ill-fitting or made of such flimsy materials that they last for only a few weeks. By and large, when we compromise on price, we get what we pay for. Over the years, many of us have become accustomed to paying relatively small sums for dresses that could pass as 'pieces' that just walked off the runways of New York, London, or Milan. But there's very little chance that the floral midi-dress you picked up for $20 could be as intricately crafted as the version Gigi Hadid wore at New York Fashion Week. If you want to reduce the churn rate in your wardrobe, instead of buying staples, such as workwear pants or winter coats, at a budget chain store, think about investing in classic, timeless looks at more upscale shops.

....

HANDLE WITH CARE

For a good part of my early twenties, I was anything but careful with my money. As a young reporter, I viewed the meager sum on my payslip as a goal to aim for, not an upper limit I ought not to reach. Looking back, I was an immature young woman who thought that a man would swoop in and take care of my financial future by marrying me. By my mid-twenties, I had a creeping sense that no knight in shining armor was going to save my finances. I'd also noticed that my spending – on knick-knacks for my bedroom, say, or ill-judged additions to my wardrobe – seemed to worsen when I was stressed out about money. And when my bank balance hit a critically low point, or even became overdrawn, I'd feel particularly deprived and hanker after furniture or a desire to throw myself into a project, all funded by my credit card.

Thankfully, before too long I realized that feeling broke had become my cue for making small, unnecessary purchases. In my case, what ended this cycle was the step of taking a €10 note from my weekly wages on payday and placing it in a jar labeled 'utilities.' It created a buffer against the feeling of being broke on those crucial days before the next payday, and had a soothing effect as I knew I could dip into it – and not deploy my credit card – if I desperately needed a little cash for small purchases such as milk or bread. Remembering after payday to replenish the jar for the sum I'd 'borrowed' became an essential part of the process. In the years since then, I've come to see money as having a quality that's like gravity.

Just as the mass of the Earth exerts a gravitational pull on objects, so money attracts a little more money.

I'd also come to see that by adopting the principle of paying myself first – by taking a sum of money from my wages and putting it away in a safe place – I'm paying due respect to the money I've earned. Over those first few days after my paycheck lands, when I see the utility companies, my insurance provider and the bank (for my mortgage) all taking their share of my money, there's comfort in knowing that one of the payments out of my account is to a savings account with my name on it. It gives me a sense of control over a precious resource; I feel like I'm handling my money with more purpose and intentionality.

Although money should never be confused with items of real value, such as the firm relationships that underpin our lives, it does remove many of the problems that can make life unbearable. And one can never underestimate the privileged position of having enough money to see one through to the next paycheck – after all, nearly 80 percent of US workers live 'paycheck to paycheck.'[40] So it makes sense to apply the principles of minimalism to this essential part of our lives.

Ask yourself: *What are my goals in relation to money? What elements of my spending result in real value, either in function or a sense of personal fulfillment? How can I be more purposeful in how I allocate the resource of money?*

Much of the time, our goals will depend on money. If your goal is to move your family to the countryside, the property transaction involved will necessarily require careful management of your resources over the next few years. If your goal is to strike out in a new career, you'll likely need savings to fund your retraining and to cover your expenses during any internships that you're obliged to undertake. If your goal is to place your life with your partner on a firmer footing, what could be a more sound foundation than removing financial cares by preparing for the future? Even if your goals aren't explicitly tied to money, it's more than likely they'll depend on having a sound financial base from which they'll grow.

The truth is, while money isn't everything, having enough money creates the conditions that help other areas of your life develop and grow to their full potential. It feels materialistic to admit it, but without giving consideration to money, it's very difficult for any aspect of our lives to thrive or even survive.

HAVE THE COURAGE TO CHANGE

Unfortunately, money is also the barometer by which society tends to measure success. And sometimes the people in our lives will judge us by this crude metric. If your friends aren't supportive of you in your attempt to simplify your life, try not to take it personally. Sometimes it's a matter of them not yet being in the mind-set to embrace change. Their priority regarding your friendship is in reassuring themselves that they're 'ahead' of you in the rat race – their version of life in the 21st century.

Buddha is credited with observing, 'When the student is ready, the teacher will come,' and it could be that your example will be the influence that makes a difference in the lives of your friends and family.

CHAPTER 4

CLEAN UP YOUR CONNECTIONS

As human beings, we're inherently social animals. From earliest childhood we reach out to those around us; we take comfort in the company of others. For most of us, it's through being with other people that we achieve personal growth, and making a new friend, forging a bond with another human being, is a heady experience. 'Each friend represents a world in us, a world possibly not born until they arrive,' wrote author Anaïs Nin, 'and it's only by this meeting that a new world is born.'

It's this strange alchemy of the heart that occurs when we meet a sympathetic soul, when we catch up with an old friend, or when we snuggle down with a loved one – we crave this and it sustains us through thick and thin. And relationships are good for us: having good relationships in your life can serve to reduce stress, help you feel part of a community, and improve your confidence. Meanwhile, as the old adage goes, a real friend is someone who walks in when the rest of the world walks out, someone who will share your good times and support you when times are bad.

If you're truly blessed, perhaps you have an *anam cara* – the Celtic 'friend of the soul,' a person to whom you can reveal the intimacies of your soul.

However, as life in the 21st century gets more complex, it can be difficult to find the time to make new friends and to cultivate the relationships we already have. People are working longer hours and face more and more demands on their free time. Meanwhile, social media, with its potential to make hundreds of friends and attract thousands of followers, is changing the nature of friendship as relationships are forged over long distances and between individuals who just a few years ago would have gone their entire lives without being aware of one another.

Friendship, no matter how it's conducted, remains the same. It's still the instant rapport between two kindred spirits who happen to have encountered each other. It's still the joy of knowing you share a lifetime's worth of memories. It'll always be the familiarity between two committed people, whether they're friends or romantic partners.

In its own way, minimalism can help foster relationships. In clearing away so much of the clutter of everyday life, at home and at work, you'll have more time to sustain the friendships, and the people, you care about the most. Simplifying your life can help assuage the guilt you perhaps feel about not attending to those relationships frequently enough. Meanwhile, minimalism can also help you cut to the heart of what your relationships mean to you, and the roles that various people play in your life. Asking probing questions of yourself – how various relationships contribute to your well-being, say, whether you've outgrown certain friendships, and whether they're worth salvaging – helps to define which of your relationships are working for you, and what you can do to save the ones you still want to retain and to nurture new friendships.

To an extent, minimalism requires you to ask how you really feel about yourself: about your personal values and about how important they are to you. Earlier, we looked at how your values inform your home life, your career choices, and your spending. But how do your fundamental values relate to the people you choose to spend your time with? As motivational speaker Jim Rohn once observed, 'You are the average of the five people you spend the most time with.' So it's time to survey the emotional landscape of your life and take stock.

WHO'S WHO IN THE FRIENDSHIP STAKES

Just as it's good practice to run the rule over our homes, stemming the flow of clutter into our lives, so it's useful for our emotional well-being to review who brings us true support and friendship. You may be surprised when you take an honest look at all of the relationships in your life.

When discussing relationships, many of us focus on intimate relationships, the relationship we have with a significant other. These provide the most meaning to our lives, and because they often form the basis of major life decisions – whether to start a family, where we'll live, how we manage our finances – intimate relationships deserve considerable attention. But it's important to take a broader look at your relationships. It's easy to forget that each of us is at the heart of our own network of personal connections. Just look at your own situation. Think of your relationships in three tiers:

THE FIRST TIER

Closest to you is your spouse or partner. If you don't have a significant other, your closest friends (usually a handful or less) and your closest family members will be in your first tier of friendship. If you're lucky, you'll count perhaps five or so people in this tier.

THE SECOND TIER

The second tier is made up of good friends, those people whose opinions you value, who cheer you on, and who are up to date on the major events in your life.

THE THIRD TIER

The third tier comprises people with whom you have a relationship but who are on the periphery of your life – neighbors, coworkers, distant family members, acquaintances you see on a regular basis.

Each tier in this model interacts with the others in a way that provides you with a complex web of support on an ongoing basis.

As the person who is closest to you, your partner will form the backbone of support in your life. Your closest friends – those who are in the first tier of friendship – also know you well and won't hesitate to give you good advice based on years, if not decades, of seeing at close quarters how you deal with problems, how you process emotions.

Meanwhile, friends just beyond this inner circle, who are in the second tier of friendship, also have our best interests at heart and will usually know how to buoy us up if we're feeling under pressure or a little low in energy.

It's worth noting that your partner, and then those in the first tier of friendship, will command more of your time and energy than those friends in the second tier, who will receive more attention than people in the third tier.

Research shows that people on the periphery of our lives, people in the third tier, nonetheless play a big role in our overall psychological well-being. A 2014 study found that having wider circles of 'weak-tie' friendships made us happier.[41] It seems that these looser connections make us feel like part of a community and reinforce feelings of inclusion in a world where busy lives make it impractical to spend time with closer friends and family.

Over the course of a lifetime, there will inevitably be movement between the tiers. Tight-knit friendships and close relationships develop over time; or, conversely, they can wither away, depending on circumstances. On the other hand, people you regard as acquaintances, or friends of friends, can become part of your inner circle.

We've seen how friendships and relationships fall into three categories. How many of these friends bring value to your life?

Who makes a positive contribution to your life?

Make a list of everybody in your life, and note into which of the three tiers described above they fall.

Then note down whether each person has a positive, negative, or neutral effect on your life.

Next, ask yourself the following questions about each person:

– Does being with them make you happy?

– Does your happiness matter to them and does it affect their behavior toward you.

– Does your relationship with them satisfy you or do you feel slightly wanting after being in their company?

– Do they help you grow?

– Do they support you when you're veering off course in challenging situations?

– Do they contribute to your life in a positive and meaningful way?

When the seven questions have been applied to each person, is your overall response that their effect on your life is positive, negative, or neutral?

You should find that you've marked the majority of your first- and second-tier relationships as 'positive.' Others have simply a neutral effect; most of the people in our peripheral third tier may well fall into this category. Whenever you encounter them, they're polite and will make small talk to pass the time. These low-stakes, low-investment relationships usually serve a purpose for both parties – they help to make workplaces run smoothly, parent-teacher councils tick over efficiently, and contribute to general low-key harmony.

Even some of our closer ties can be listed as having a neutral effect on our lives. For example, you may have close relatives you don't especially gel with but whom you know would have your back in a time of crisis. Our ongoing relationships with these family members could be described as 'neutral' without causing much offence.

For the most part, all your relationships will nurture you, make you feel more secure in the world.

They'll be a source of strength on those occasions when life throws you a curveball. These relationships have a positive net effect on your life: the lover who brings you a cup of tea in bed, the old friend who will always put a smile on your face after a long day at work, the colleague who marks your birthday by leaving a cupcake on your desk. Then there's the barista who smiles and greets you by name in your local coffee shop, the retired lady who says hello when you pass each other in the park, and the nice woman whose children are friends with your children – they all feed into this network of positivity in our social world.

Meanwhile, there can be relationships in any of the tiers that can be described as having a negative effect. These relationships drain us of energy; they bring out our worst traits, and the thought of spending time with those people fills us with dread and low-level anxiety. Sometimes these relationships can be negotiated only on whatever terms the other party is capable of, or even come to an end.

Third-tier relationships that have an overall negative effect are manageable. Encountering such people can be tricky even where the environment is so structured that meaningful contact is minimized – say, in a workplace or at a family gathering. However, such meetings can be made easier if you know that you have first- and second-tier relationships in your life that are on a more sure footing.

It's when our closer relationships – those with people in the first tier – are negative that we need to take a closer look at our lives.

Many of these individuals form the core of our support group, and feel part of who we are, so any negative effect is bound to be unnerving, if not destabilizing. We also depend on many of the people in the second tier of relationships for forms of support and guidance. If their overall effect on our lives is negative, either the nature of the relationship must change, or the person gets a red card.

A CHANGE OF SCENE

In the 21st century, there's a feeling that we and the makeshift 'family' of friends we've gathered around us are bound together in an unbreakable unit; that the friends we made in school or in our early twenties should be the tribe we travel with through the rest of our lives. And that 'losing' such friends along the way should be a source of shame.

But people change. There's the woman you went with to South America on your gap year twenty-five years ago, who has different priorities now that she's married with two young children, and she may care little for your struggles in the world of dating. Perhaps there's a school friend who has acquired questionable political opinions in the years since you hung out together and is now somebody you can no longer bear.

And if our friends have changed, there's a good chance that we've changed too, and that our older friends may find it difficult to relate to our new selves.

Sometimes, where the friendship is foundering due to lack of contact, just spending time together in a relaxed atmosphere can get things back on track.

If there's goodwill on both sides, making time just for an afternoon coffee, with outside commitments forgotten for an hour or so, can be enough to halt the sense of drift.

Sometimes the real issue is that the friendship has simply deteriorated over the years, perhaps due to resentments building up on one or both sides. If you find that your attempts to arrange a date to meet are being repeatedly rebuffed, it may be time to quietly call a halt to the relationship. Accept that future contact will be limited to liking one another's posts on social media, and move on.

Of greater concern are the friends who bring little value to your table. Instead of being a source of richness and meaning, they leave us emotionally drained, or play favorites, or appear in our lives only when they want something. Sometimes the realization can creep up on us over a matter of months or years, but occasionally it can hit us like a thunderbolt – the sickening sensation that the person we once counted on as a friend doesn't have our best interests at heart. Or that a person we regarded as a kindred spirit is no longer the man or woman we thought they were. It's a jarring feeling, knowing that a friendship has turned sour.

Unfortunately, such friendships can stagger on for years, sustained by the thin gruel of alcohol-fueled nights out and breathless catch-ups filled with toxic gossip about other sometime friends. Within these semi-functional relationships, there can be fault on both sides. Sometimes having so-called 'frenemies' allows us to give free rein to a side of our personality we're not proud of, or even gives us an insight into a lifestyle we don't approve of. If you feel that a relationship is leaving you feeling empty, a little used, or slightly soiled because you're letting yourself down, you need to take action.

BIRDS OF A FEATHER

The most important element of a friendship, or any form of meaningful relationship, is having shared values. If our values are at odds with a so-called friend's, the relationship won't feel right. This lack of harmony can be glaring: say, if you care deeply about the environment but your friend buys a new car every year; if you've been maintaining a minimalist home and your friend treats shopping like an Olympic sport she's training for, it'll be difficult to maintain a friendship based on mutual interests.

A lack of shared values can emerge in other ways, too. If your friendship has been merely surviving over a period of years on a meager diet of sporadic text messages and a few brief words when meeting within a large group, it can come as a shock to discover that somebody you regard as a friend has a habit of talking down mutual friends, or harbors views that are sexist or racist.

Even if our friends lead very different lives to us – even if they're immersed in parenthood while we're caring for elderly relatives – there should be values that we have in common; that you both have a profound belief in the importance of family, say, or that you're both committed to lives of integrity and honesty.

Shared values will transcend circumstances,
maintaining a bond that will form the
basis of the strongest friendship.

WALK THE WALK

Of course, the values we hold are only as sincere as the values we live by. When we talk about being committed to the environment but buy a multi-pack of bottled mineral water; when we claim to value loyalty but can't be bothered to travel for a friend's birthday party – in such instances we fail to live up to our own values. We create a cognitive dissonance, a jarring sense of disconnect, between how we know we should behave and what we actually do. So check in with yourself, and consider whether you've been following your own code of conduct. If you've veered off course in recent years, perhaps it's time to figure out how to reconcile yourself with the values that really matter to you.

Sometimes our values and beliefs simply have to be discarded. For example, for many years I held quite conservative values; I simply believed that life had been better in the old days. But the more I saw of life, the more I learnt about what life had in fact been like for women and children in 'the good old days,' the more I saw that my desire to turn back the clock to a 'simpler' time was ill-informed. I found that I had to rethink my values, something that took effort and time. But good friends were patient with me, and provided me with the emotional space I needed to process the dissonance between my old values and the facts. I was eventually able to achieve growth and look at the world with a fresh perspective.

Sometimes our own values change, and those of our friends do not, and vice versa.

But occasionally there's such a mismatch between the values of ourselves and our friends that the distance between us can never be recovered. If there's a lasting unease between you and the first- or second-tier friends from whom you detect a negative effect, ask yourself if this boils down to not sharing the same set of values. And is this clash of values enough to make you rethink these relationships?

OUT WITH THE OLD

When we see that some relationships are falling short, we sometimes believe that we must still stick with these friends – not out of a sense of loyalty but because we fear we won't make any other friends, as if relationships are a finite resource that can run out. But anybody can make new friends at any time.

You may believe that 'making friends' is a skill that you simply don't have. We all know people who appear to glide through life collecting new friends along the way. But if you study such people, you inevitably find that many of their gifts for making friends are due to habits they've honed over the years. Is your friend Rachel blessed with genius-level intelligence, or is she interesting to talk with because she follow the news and goes to the cinema from time to time? Is Nathan innately charismatic, or does he just listen carefully to the person he's speaking with, then respond confidently and politely?

Perhaps you believe that the opportunities for making new friends dry up as we go through life. When we're in our teens and early twenties, the potential for meeting like-minded individuals is boundless. Between school, gap years, university, clubs, hobbies, work and holidays, hundreds, if not thousands, of people pass through our lives. By the time we reach our late twenties, when life has steadied a little and we have commitments that make it hard to sustain a vibrant social life, it can feel like the scope for meeting new people, let alone make new friends, has diminished to the point where it's simply not worth the effort.

But once you've organized your friends and family into the three tiers, you may find that relationships you regard as peripheral, say at work or church, are more meaningful and rewarding than some of the supposedly closer bonds that you forged in your personal life decades ago.

Sometimes the people in those peripheral relationships become friends without you realizing it.

IN WITH THE NEW

I found myself in just such a situation a few years ago after I spotted a small notice in my local supermarket that read: 'Volunteers wanted.' A charity was looking for people to join its roster of people who pay visits to the elderly. The appearance of this sign, not much bigger than a postcard, came just at the right time. I was in a job that was both boring and frustrating. Even worse, it leached out into my personal time.

Over the previous years my social circle had grown smaller and smaller. My family were on the other side of the country and my unusual working hours meant that it was difficult to see them. So I signed up with this charity's befriending service, where I'd be helping to ease a pensioner's loneliness by calling in once a week.

After the training and police vetting, eventually I was paired with a recently widowed man named Tommy. 'He's eighty-three,' said the lady from the charity, 'and he's lovely!' She wasn't wrong. Tommy is 'a relic of auld decency,' to borrow an old Irish phrase. He religiously follows the fortunes of the Ireland rugby team, he loves listening to Pavarotti records, and his driving passion is researching the history of the First World War. In short, we have no interests in common. Yet, in the six years since I started visiting Tommy, our friendship has become one of the most meaningful relationships in my life.

Every Wednesday, I call round at 8 p.m. Until recently, we'd sit at the kitchen table and enjoy mugs of tea and slices of fruitcake slathered in butter. But thanks to the diabetes nurse we now content ourselves with just the mugs of tea. It doesn't matter. We still sit at Tommy's kitchen table and set the world to rights. He'll ask after my family, try against the odds to educate me about Irish rugby, and without judging me he'll offer advice about how to tackle tricky situations that arise in life. Over the years, my friendship with Tommy has highlighted everything that set other friendships off course.

Meanwhile, I found that for Tommy, making new connections is a lifelong pursuit. After a stay in hospital that put our visits on pause, Tommy was able to tell me about the friends he'd made in the hospital, and about the long lunch he'd taken earlier that week with another new friend who is decades younger than he is.

After nine decades on Earth (he turned 90 in 2019), Tommy reasons that every person he meets is basically a decent human being.

He will treat everybody he meets as if they have the same values – belief in the family, the merits of hard work, the importance of ordinary decency toward all others – until they demonstrate otherwise.

Tommy may not be familiar with the finer points of minimalism but he has a deep understanding of the essence of friendship: that shared values go a long way toward creating meaningful bonds that will stand the test of time, and that generosity of spirit can lead to conversations where real friendships can take root, and perhaps even blossom.

If you accept that many people, in many areas of your life, are open to friendship, you'll see the many opportunities for either meeting new people or for developing more rewarding relationships with people who are already somewhere in your life, even if they're currently on its periphery. They could be the friend of a friend who has just moved to your neighborhood, the mother who drops off her children at school at the same time as you... or they could be an elderly man you meet through charity work.

LOOKING BACK – AND FORWARD

The wonderful thing about human relationships is that they're fluid. They adapt according to the circumstances; they're as flexible as we are. If you've had poor relationships in the past, this doesn't mean you're destined to continue to have bad relationships as you go into the future. If a relationship has left you feeling lost, unhappy with yourself, or disappointed, then take comfort in the fact that you can learn from the experience and move on, ready to make new relationships that provide you with the emotional nourishment you need and where you're valued as a phenomenal human being who contributes to the world.

Your past need not define you.

If you choose, you can look back at previous friendships and relationships that fell short of your needs, analyze them and work out what went wrong. It can be emotionally painful to relive the hurts and slights that chipped away at us, and chastening to recall how we behaved badly and let ourselves down. It can seem easier to simply throw ourselves into buying the latest cookbooks or a bottle of expensive perfume. But taking a non-judgmental look at the past – noting which behaviors were helpful, and which habits led to the toxic aspects of our interactions – can be instructive in how we lay down the foundations of healthy friendships and relationships that will sustain us in the future.

As you move on from the emotional landscape that's been failing you, and travel toward a point of greater fulfillment, you'll be armed with greater self-knowledge and self-awareness. Be aware of what worked in the past, and what didn't work; identify how you can spot people with similar values and attitudes; and recognize how valuable friendships characterized by respect and affection grew out of merely passing connections.

When you make friendships that meet your needs, your existing friends may raise their game as they see the changes in you.

If you prioritize your own life, you may find you prompt a rethink in friends who have perhaps drifted or allowed trivial interests to clutter up their own lives. If you feel that these sometime friends have undergone a sea change in their thinking, accept the hand of friendship if it's extended to you. Life is a series of lessons, and if we can learn to reboot our attitudes to friendships, it would be churlish to reject the efforts made by people who may themselves be on a journey of self-knowledge.

The same is equally pertinent when it comes to romantic relationships. It's important to remember that just because a relationship turned sour in the past, you're not destined to live a life of loneliness forever. You always have the power to create a better future – starting now.

Sometimes, the most devastating legacy of an unhealthy relationship can be a creeping fear of getting close to anybody ever again. Heartbreakingly, this can manifest itself in behavior that will push away other potential friends and lovers. If you've been burnt in the past, are you running from situations where new friendships may arise? When you meet someone new, are you covering your insecurities and fears in a patina of busyness and surface-level banter designed to deflect meaningful conversations?

As we reach our thirties and forties, as family commitments and working lives get in the way of regular socializing, we often tell ourselves, 'I don't have time for new friends,' but making friends and maintaining friendships should be a lifelong process. After all, when we emerge from those hectic years of night feeds, school runs, serving as a taxi driver for teenagers, dispatching a young man or woman into adult life... we want to have a circle of friends to call on. (The good news is that many of your old friends are going through the same process, and you should be able to pick up the threads of those friendships when your lives calm down a little.)

THE GIFT OF FRIENDSHIP

Presenting gifts is one of life's greatest pleasures. Very little compares to the joy of seeing a friend's face light up as they unwrap a gift that you chose for them with love. But buying gifts can also become an area fraught with anxiety, particularly if you've embraced a minimalist lifestyle and your friends haven't.

Too many people confuse lavish with thoughtful, or expensive with well chosen. Having grown up in a culture in which our self-worth is tied to how much we earn – or perhaps, more accurately, the extent to which our lifestyles telegraph wealth and success to our peers – we've all seen instances where gift-giving has virtually become a competitive sport.

If you're embarking on a journey into minimalism, explain your new mind-set to your friends. Remind them that, sometimes, bigger isn't better. And sometimes, an expensive present doesn't fully fit in with the lifestyle of the person receiving it. (I've also found that getting a loved one a big-ticket item, such as a camera or a computer tablet, denies them the experience of researching what's on the market, evaluating the various features, and so on. If you feel like playing bountiful godparent to a younger person, check yourself before you swoop in to 'solve their problem' by throwing money at it.)

It's lovely to be generous with friends and family
but that generosity may be misdirected.

Sit down with the intended recipient and get to the heart of what they actually want. Perhaps they would prefer a cash contribution toward their next purchase, or perhaps they would simply prefer a little more of your time.

My friend Olive made the decision years ago to make 'A fun day out with Aunty Olive' her gift to her nieces and nephews. This involved taking them out for a grown-up meal and then going to a festive pantomime. 'It would definitely be cheaper to simply buy something out of a catalogue for them,' says Olive, 'but they already have everything they could possibly need, in material terms. And I like to think that I'm creating memories that we'll all treasure in the future.' She knows that the day will come when her nieces and nephews will be too old and too cool to want to hang out with their Aunty Olive, but when that happens, Olive says, she'll simply give them the freedom to have a fun day out with their own friends by giving them cinema or theatre vouchers.

AFFAIRS OF THE HEART

It's been said that the very best romantic relationships begin in the realm of friendship. But many relationships also depend on the alchemy of sparking contrasts. He loves salsa dancing; you'd rather be at the cinema watching the latest release. You live for the weekend when you go hiking together; he looks forward to the takeout he'll grab on the way home. The important thing is that there's respect on both sides – that you can appreciate your partner's passion for a 1990s indie band or obsession with flea markets, and they can do the same for your love of vintage radio sets and kayaking. Ultimately, it's differences like these that give relationships a little spice and provide the emotional space that allows a passionate relationship to continue to grow.

With your home free of clutter, your work goals clear and your finances in check, how does your primary relationship look? If minimalism is about stripping away extraneous objects and annoying distractions, a healthy relationship is about permitting enough intimacy to fully drop one's guard, and allowing your partner to see the real you. It's about engaging with each other with honesty and trust, and truly communicating – not just about the logistics of your household, but about the issues that are weighing you down. Your relationship will be characterized by caring actions and authenticity. It'll also involve no small degree of understanding – a willingness to see the other person's point of view, and a respect for the other partner's decisions.

Making space in your lives for your relationship should also mean making time for each other, even where family obligations threaten to encroach. We hear much talk about 'quality time' in a relationship, but it's difficult to achieve quality time if you're not willing to commit time to going for a meal or taking a walk. In years to come, it'll be the shared moments that will live longest in the memory.

THE DATING GAME

Perhaps you've been burnt by love in the past. If you feel ready to dip a toe in the dating waters once more, first figure out what you really want. Do you want a soul mate, or do you want a playmate?

Do you want a relationship with somebody who can slot into your life as it stands, or do you want to strike out on a completely new adventure?

We can sometimes come under pressure to conform to the set ideals of what a relationship should look like, but if you've been applying the principles of minimalism to your home life, your work goals and your finances, you'll have the emotional clarity to weigh up exactly what you want from a relationship, and what form it should take.

Some people have reported that minimalism helped them free up the emotional energy required to launch themselves into dating life. Others have said that decluttering their homes forced them to discard the little keepsakes that were keeping alive the memories of previous relationships. As you re-enter the dating world, allow the clarity of mind that's marked your journey in minimalism to remain your constant ally. Certainly, try to drop all preconceptions, and guard against being judgmental about potential partners, but remain mindful of how you expend your energy, and be clear – to yourself, at any rate – about your goal. The most helpful mind-set is to embark on your dating journey with a healthy sense of adventure. See where the journey takes you, and who you get to take with you for the ride!

VENTURING ONLINE

I can still remember signing up to Facebook for the first time. It was early 2007 and I'd been reading articles about this new phenomenon. However, I was so early to the party that the only person I could find on Facebook was a woman who had attended my old school, about three years ahead of me. She probably had only the vaguest memory of who I was, but she accepted my friend invitation. Neither of us could have known that within a year, Facebook would become a powerful, all-consuming force potentially connecting each of us with more than two billion other people. Today, Facebook is just one social media platform; it's been joined by Instagram and Twitter, now also vital tools of communication in the 21st century.

However, a 2016 study found that those of us who have a large cohort of friends on social media report that, in real life, they turn to just a handful of people for support. Oxford psychology professor Robin Dunbar (who devised 'Dunbar's number,' or the theory that most people will find it difficult to maintain stable social relationships with more than 150 people) found that cultivating large circles of 'friends' on Facebook didn't result in greater numbers of good friends; it just led to people redefining the term 'friend' to justify the inclusion of more and more people into their online friendship networks.[42]

Even if curating ever-larger numbers of friends online doesn't make a difference to the number of genuinely close friends we have, there's some evidence that the overall emotional effect of engaging in a social platform touted as a way of promoting interpersonal connections is an increased feeling of loneliness.

It's the ultimate paradox: how to have hundreds of friends and yet feel as if you have nobody to turn to.

Studies vary in their conclusions as to whether Facebook contributes to loneliness. According to one 2011 report, lonely people spend more time on the social media platform than non-lonely people do, and their use of Facebook is characterized by passive scrolling through posts rather than interacting with other users.[43] According to a 2010 study, when users interact with posts – say, by 'liking' linked articles, or commenting on status updates – they experience enhanced feelings of connection and less loneliness. Meanwhile, Facebook users who content themselves with merely scrolling down through posts, with no interaction, report lower feelings of connection with their online friends and increased levels of loneliness.[44, 45]

Depending on social media alone to fulfill our needs in relation to friendship and companionship is a losing battle against loneliness. Social media is useful if you're parted from friends over an extended period, but it's a poor substitute for actually sitting down with an old pal and spending some time with them. Meanwhile, the ease and low-friction nature of hitting the 'like' button can lead to a false sense of emotional intimacy and contact. I've lost count of the number of times I warmly saluted a virtual stranger in real life just because we engaged in ritually 'liking' each other's tweets. At least they only led to fleeting embarrassment. What's worse – much worse – were the occasions when I assumed that all was well in a friend's life (when it wasn't) simply because their social media feed gave the impression of a flawless existence, free of problems.

Ask yourself, have you made the mistake of idly 'liking' a friend's status update and continuing to scroll through the rest of your social media feeds instead of fixing a date to go for coffee? Or just picking up the phone and making a call? Try to get into the routine of reaching out to people in your first- and second-tier groups of friends on a more regular basis, or even sending a private message instead of telegraphing your affection by way of a 'like' on social media.

Ultimately, meaningful connection with another person – preferably in the context of real-life, one-on-one contact – is what we all crave in life. After all, loneliness has serious consequences for our health. A 10-year study of 12,000 people by Florida State University found that being lonely could increase your risk of dementia by 40 percent.[46] One remarkable takeaway from the study was that loneliness couldn't be predicted: feeling lonely wasn't conditional on the number of social contacts one had. So, one can be surrounded by people and yet still feel lonely.

Relationships, whether they be acquaintances, friendships, or loving, life-long partnerships, have the potential to be sources of great joy… or great pain. If we're privileged enough to find true friends, we may be lucky enough to catch a glimpse into another person's soul. But if we allow ourselves to become caught up in other people's toxic dramas, or allow ourselves to slip into old, unhelpful relationship patterns, we'll find it difficult to thrive and grow as people.

So, make the time to evaluate the relationship landscape of your life. Who are the friends who are supportive? Who are the friends who see the person you could be, who will cheer you on in your journey to become the most evolved version of yourself? Resolve to invest more of your time and energy where you find wells of respect and support.

CHAPTER 5

REGULATE YOUR (VIRTUAL) REALITY

It's amazing that just 20 years ago, the Internet was something that 'lived' in your work PC or possibly in your home computer – if the chirping, crackling gods of dial-up smiled upon you. It's difficult to remember now, but for a number of years, from the late 1990s onward, the Internet was where you went merely to send an email, track down a recipe, or rant on a message board. Nobody was prepared for the revolution in 2007 when Apple's Steve Jobs launched the first iPhone. The iPhone wasn't the first smartphone, but it led the way in fully opening up access to the Internet for the masses.

As has been well documented elsewhere, the genius touch was allowing developers to build and share apps that gave the smartphone true functionality while on the move. It meant that the power of the Internet was now in your pocket, not just on your office desk or in the spare room at home.

More than a decade on, we're still adjusting to the shift in mind-set. Most people over the age of 30 have a clear recall of what life was like before smartphones, when pub arguments about major sporting achievements couldn't be settled by a flick of the wrist and the appearance of a smartphone, and when a route to an unfamiliar area had to be plotted on a paper map and noting down the directions.

But on the cusp of the third decade of the 21st century, smartphones and social media are firmly part of our lives, and there seems to be no way back from it. By 2016 more websites were being accessed by mobile devices than desktop computers.

But super-convenient computer access comes at a price.

The advertising industry has leapt on this opportunity to deliver its wares literally into the hands of potential consumers, diverting vast sums of ad revenue by advertising their product on popular apps and websites, quickly bringing results. Consider what it meant to advertisers that by 2018 Facebook had attracted more than 2 billion users.

What's more, online platforms, particularly Facebook, can help advertisers target their advertisements to specific demographic groups, thanks to the data that we, as users, have unwittingly disclosed during our online interactions. Every 'like' we bestowed on a favorite band, every competition we entered in the hope of winning a $100 voucher for one of our favorite stores, every time we took issue with an extreme political stance as expressed by a relative – they can potentially all be collated as data ready to be fed back to commercial interests.

There's now a tacit expectation that everybody is available to communicate at any point during waking hours, if not beyond that.

If you have a smartphone – and today nearly everybody is expected to have a smartphone – your employer may expect you to download an app that will allow you to be accessible by email at all times. (It's possible that your employer won't expect you to reply or process the email when you're away from your desk, but this does little to quell the feeling of dismay when an email detailing a customer complaint slips into your phone's inbox on your day off.) And how often have you fibbed, 'Sorry – only seeing this now....' as you finally formulated a response to a friend's message sent via Facebook messenger. But we're aware that not having the time, energy, or emotional capacity to deal with a message straight away – even when the query isn't time sensitive – may be perceived by the other party as being deliberately incommunicado, so we ramp up the pressure on ourselves to reply straight away, rather than take time to deliberate. No wonder you're exhausted so much of the time!

That's why it's time to step off the treadmill. If the minimalist lifestyle is about clearing your life of the clutter that gets in the way of living an intentional life, does it make any sense to have a piece of brushed steel and polished glass play such a central role in it? If we truly value simplicity in our surroundings and in our relationships, why are we complicating things with a device that shows us the melees playing out online every minute? It's time for a reboot.

A BLESSING AND A CURSE

I can't be the only person who finds that social media can be both a blessing and a curse. On the one hand, it's given me access to people I'd never have made contact with. In a few weeks from now, I'll travel to a comedy gig in a city 125 miles away with a woman I 'met' over social media. I say met, but we haven't actually met in real life. All we know is that we have the same taste in early 1990s comedians, and that we're both up for a bit of adventure.

Social media has succeeded in rewriting
the rules of communication.

Friendships can be forged on the basis of shared interests – a beloved TV show, a genre of fiction, a love of French cuisine – rather than physical proximity. Meanwhile, information no longer goes in one direction only: the days of a small coterie of media editors deciding what should formulate the news agenda, and then issuing the news via a relatively small number of newspapers or broadcasts, now seems hopelessly outdated. Thanks to technology, individuals decide their own news agenda to find out how politicians are spending taxpayers' money, how vast corporations are running their businesses, or even just how their favorite actor is spending their downtime. The truly revolutionary aspect to this is that now we, as taxpayers, consumers, or simply fans, can ourselves communicate in real time with politicians, companies, or celebrities via social media, truly opening up a meaningful dialog with power.

Social media can provide a cozy sense of community, present you with the opportunity to strike out and find your tribe, or even advocate for a cause you feel strongly about.

However, it can also be a miserable place. Just a few weeks ago, I witnessed an intelligent and good man verbally eviscerated online after posting a thoughtful blog post about excessive traffic in his neighborhood. It was painful to watch an anonymous stranger take this man to task, resorting to abusive language as he honed in on a passage of the blog that was slightly dismissive of cyclists, and willfully misinterpreted a tangential paragraph of fewer than 40 words. 'How are you doing?' I asked the recipient of the verbal attack a few hours after being told to 'piss off' by the nameless Twitter user. He replied: 'I feel like I've literally been knocked sideways.'

It was a reminder that in this age of hyperconnectivity, where we can have hundreds of friends and thousands of followers, there are people who won't hesitate to give vent to their aggression by abusing strangers on the Internet who express views that are slightly different from their own.

It's not surprising, then, that instead of disclosing our more strident views, or using social media as an instrument of self-expression, many of us choose to 'snack' on social media, grazing on snapshots of other people's lives and idly picking over the issues of the day. These feel like safe interactions with the world beyond our virtual front door. And these low-stakes maneuvers, such as scrolling down your Facebook app on the commute to work or checking in on the Instagram stories of celebrities, require much lower investments of energy than telephoning the friend you haven't seen in a while or reading the latest book by your favorite author.

However, it's very easy to fall into the trap of believing that benevolently issuing 'likes' to our Facebook friends shores up real relationships in our offline world.

Your closest and most healthy
relationships require more than a friendly
'thumbs up' to sustain them.

The healthiest friendships grow out of a vibrant interplay of personal chemistry and common interests, but they can flourish only where there's mutual respect, ongoing communication, and a commitment to finding time to be emotionally present, to be there for one another. When people cultivate large networks of Facebook friends, it simply isn't possible for them to relate to hundreds of people with any level of closeness. For the majority of our Facebook friends, most of our interactions are on the same footing as a friendly wave to a neighbor or a little friendly banter with a coworker – actions that help create goodwill, but not the sort of high-energy commitment that cements relationships.

As a way of fostering actual friendships
in real life, Facebook and other forms of
social media have their limitations.

That's not to say that online friendships can't make the transition into relationships in real life, but they require a commitment of energy and time to manage the maneuver.

However, more and more research shows that spending more time on social media leaves us feeling empty and unfulfilled. Comparing our existence to friends' and acquaintances' Facebook posts of the glossiest versions of their lives is associated with feelings of low self-esteem and can lead to 'poorer well-being.'[47] In one study, published in 2018, people reduced the time they spent on platforms such as Instagram and Facebook over a three-week period, and reported feeling less lonely, less depressed, less anxious, and less subject to the so-called 'fear of missing out.'[48] In the same study, students who were tasked with simply limiting their use of social media also found they had lower levels of anxiety and of the fear of missing out. Meanwhile, a study published in 2016 showed that people who were users of between seven and 11 social media outlets 'had more than three times the risk of depression and anxiety' than people who used two or fewer platforms.[49]

Surprised?

I didn't think so. Almost anybody who has encountered social media will be familiar with the nagging feeling that spending time on Facebook or Instagram, or any online platform where real life can be polished and Photoshopped to within an inch of its life, has the potential to create as much unhappiness as joy.

Although most of us are guilty of indulging in this shameless display of exhibitionism, when we ourselves are on holiday or 'humblebragging' about our achievements, it can be all too easy to give in to an urge to compare our humdrum lives with the filtered pictures from somebody else's highlights reel: the snap of a cocktail taken at a hotel poolside, captioned, 'Just another day at the office...,' the selfie taken on an awe-inspiring mountaintop by your gym buddy, or the relative who smugly posts a picture of the dozens of perfectly iced cupcakes they've prepared for the school cake sale.

Just like Pizza Friday at the office, these low-stakes 'grazing' sessions leave us feeling bloated and uncomfortable, yet curiously we find ourselves looking for more of the same. They don't use much energy, yet they draw on our psychological reserves in a manner that makes us unsettled and restless. But we're not alone.

WHY SCROLLING IS ADDICTIVE

The typical smartphone user touches their phone 2,167 times per day; the 2016 research mentioned above found that some people check in with their device over 5,000 times per day,[50] while in 2018 the average US user spent 3 hours and 23 minutes per day on their device.[51]

The reason? Social media is 'sticky': once the smartphone is in your hand and you're scrolling through Facebook or Twitter posts, it becomes difficult to put down.

> The fragments of life we glimpse on an
> Instagram selfie, a Facebook status, or a
> Twitter update, leave us hungry for more.

They offer just enough information to entice us to buy into whatever is going on in our friends' lives and endeavor to learn more details.

Facebook, in particular, was designed to have this 'sticky' quality. The company's founding president, Sean Parker, disclosed in 2017 that, in its earliest days, Facebook's designers were set the task of maximizing the amount of time users spent on the website. According to Parker (who has since left the company), the objective was: 'How do we consume as much of your time and conscious attention as possible?'[52]

It was a similar thought process that inspired the development of the 'Like' button: it encouraged engagement and made interaction with a friend's page something that could be played out in front of all your mutual friends. Meanwhile, for the person posting a cute picture or a thoughtful observation about life, the 'Like' button became a little pat on the back, an endorsement of one's good taste or opinions. 'It's a social-validation feedback loop,' Mr. Parker said. 'Exactly the kind of thing that a hacker like myself would come up with, because you're exploiting a vulnerability in human psychology.'[53]

It's true that every time we engage with social media by 'sharing' something from our lives, we reveal a little about ourselves, leaving us open to the silent judgment of our friends and acquaintances, and making us vulnerable to verbal attack. Will our friends share in our good fortune at finally taking a holiday, even if the location isn't one they'd choose themselves? Will they overlook the shiny forehead and pimply skin that the midhike selfie shows off so well? Will they accept that, as people, we're growing and that opinions we once held dear have changed over the years?

Meanwhile, as consumers, we experience the buzz of anticipation for uncertain rewards. Checking out our Twitter feed is like spinning a roulette wheel. Who knows what will pop up after we hit refresh? Just take the last three actions on my Twitter feed: a cute video of a dog being reunited with his owners after being lost for two months; an invitation to meet a friend for coffee; and a news story about the partial destruction of a wildlife reserve. What a rollercoaster ride of emotions! But when our own everyday lives can seem a little humdrum, the opportunity to access a little cuteness overload, arrange a coffee date or feel as if we're engaging with the world at large – and all at the touch of a button – can be too tempting to turn down.

Ultimately, when we're mindlessly scrolling through our various social media feeds late at night, well aware that we could instead be using this time to work through our dozens of tasks, it can feel very much as if we're in the grip of a compulsion that's not serving our best interests.

SELLING OUR SOULS

The truth is that snacking on social media provides us with just enough of a feeling of community and warmth that we feel sustained just enough for the short term. But in our search for self-validating 'likes' or our campaign to keep abreast of distant acquaintances' garden makeovers, we're not only feasting on a diet that fails to meet our needs but also feeding industry's insatiable hunger for data on our tastes and interests so that advertisers can aim directly at us.

Over the past decade, big business has been made from harvesting your data then trying to sell you products you think you need. Billions of dollars have been invested in trying to uncover information about what clothes we like to buy, which theater shows we go to, which sports teams we support.

Who knew that when Orwell wrote 'Big Brother is watching you,' Big Brother's interests would run to something as mundane as our shopping baskets?

As we've learnt in recent years, our online habits also may have become political tools. In the USA in 2016, consumers' online lives were dissected for political gain when data harvested from up to 87 million Facebook users without their knowledge was used in a closely run presidential campaign to target potential voters. In the wake of the Cambridge Analytica data scandal, as the affair became known, Facebook CEO Mark Zuckerberg made efforts to ensure a similar breach can't happen again, but the episode spurred many people to weigh up the importance of social media in their lives. As we're learning to appreciate, when the product is free, you – the user – are the product. Your data becomes the price you pay for the privilege of using a website or app.

So while Facebook, Twitter, and Instagram can help us create a sense of community, and to keep in touch with friends who live far away from us, social media can also leave us feeling anxious, depressed, and with lower feelings of self-worth as we compare ourselves unfavorably to others. On top of this, it also supplies businesses with valuable marketing data.

If you feel weak and miserable for getting caught up in this cycle, don't. Just ask yourself why you're mindlessly snacking on social media. Once you disentangle yourself from the psychological 'hacking' to which you've been subjecting yourself over the past decade, what are the benefits to being on Facebook, Instagram, or Twitter? Is this really the best use of your time?

As we considered in Chapter 1: does it bring value to your life?

SOCIAL CLUTTER

Ultimately, much of our engagement with social media falls under the heading of 'clutter.' And as we've seen elsewhere, clutter ends up draining your time and energy. It gets in the way of your life, doing largely nothing useful, permitted to stay there on the off-chance that some day it'll come into its own. It's the same with social media. Perhaps, some day, somebody will post on your Facebook timeline an article that will change your life. Perhaps, some day, the love of your life will double-click your picture on Instagram, you'll fall in love with each other straight away and live happily ever after. Perhaps, some day, using the power of logic in an online discussion, you'll manage to change the mind of that bigot you follow on Twitter. The problem with these scenarios is that while they might happen some day, you'll have wasted thousands of hours of your life waiting for them to appear.

Meanwhile, most of us use social media on our mobile devices in the same way that a baby uses a pacifier. We pick up our smartphones when we're bored or tired. But cast your mind back a few years to your childhood: remember when being bored was a regular occurrence? When access to TV was limited by both the restrictions set by your parents and the small number of channels? When the summer holidays were characterized not by a full roster of summer camp activities but by long days filled with nothing to do? When long car journeys were marked by games of 'I Spy,' not playing games on an iPad.

People forget how useful boredom can be.

The state of boredom can be fertile ground for creativity or an innovative approach to problem-solving. How many skipping games were made up on the spot because we were bored? How many times did we improvise new lyrics to much-loved songs because we were bored? How often was a flair discovered for a previously unknown talent because we were bored?

According to psychologist Sherry Turkle, 'Boredom is your imagination calling to you.'[54] It's the clarion call from your subconscious to do something that will change your circumstances. It's the whispered message from your inner self, urging you to pick up that book once more. It's the impulse to do something, anything, that will stimulate your brain – not something that will bombard it with visual stimulation and leave it exhausted.

This isn't to say that we should try to turn back the
clock to a time before smartphones and social media.

As we've seen, social media can be a remarkable tool for fostering community and helping to forge friendships. But the key word in that sentence is 'tool': social media should be used to help us as users; we shouldn't be in others' service through social media. Ask yourself at what point does social media – or the use of your digital devices – stop being something you're using with intentionality, and become something that you should simply park.

KNOW WHAT'S HEALTHY

I must confess that I'm not very discerning in who I follow on Twitter – I'm as much a sucker for a backstage selfie at a glitzy awards ceremony as anybody else – but the people I return to again and again are people who are judicious in how they themselves use the medium. They include the political activist who can skewer the arguments of climate change deniers in two sentences; the comedy writer whose whimsical tweets make me want to buy her a coffee (or her next book); the journalist who can explain a complex story in 280 characters.

But many users take a scattergun approach to their tweets. They use Twitter as a place to vent about an item they just heard on the radio, to pass on garbled information they picked up somewhere (possibly via social media), or to lambast the wardrobe choices of a celebrity sitting in sweatpants that should have been laundered three days ago. Most people fail to appreciate that the world isn't waiting with bated breath for their commentary on any given day's burning issue in current affairs.

Many people who admit to creeping exhaustion in their dealings with social media are failing to approach the platform with an air of intentionality.

They may find themselves reacting to every inflammatory post, or trying to anticipate the mood within their own 'tribe' by retweeting an ill-judged comment with a cutting remark that mocks the witless tweeter. But this level of surveillance, with the Twitterati perpetually ready to jump in and offer their own hot take on the next media row, doesn't help matters. Tweeters whose arguments either miss the point or drive it home with a sledgehammer quickly swamp relevant and sensitively worded contributions. More and more, I find that my main Twitter feed is a bewildering and angry place.

So I've begun curating a list of users I know in real life. I find that they're less trigger-happy, less inclined to fire broadsides at 'the government,' or to trade in conspiracy theories. In addition, the personal news that they tweet about – and which I'm far more invested in – is less likely to become subsumed in the deluge of strangers' rants about the latest political crisis.

As a way of staying abreast of news and current affairs, social media is of only limited use. For one thing, it's not always immediately clear whether the news source is reliable or unbiased, unless the post has been issued by an established newspaper or broadcaster, or by a proper journalist.

Scrolling down through a timeline, grabbing snippets of news, can have the effect of making us feel both overwhelmed by events and powerless to act.

A better solution might be to read a properly researched newspaper or magazine article in full, and contribute to resolving the situation by joining forces with a charity or political party where you can make a real difference.

Given the problematic nature of, say, Twitter, as a news source, it's perhaps no surprise that some people find it useful to place time limits on when they'll interact with social media. In alignment with minimalist principles, they see the value of social media as a means of, say, raising their profile. So they'll post an article that's relevant to their professional interests and engage politely with whoever takes the time to leave a comment. They may even get a feel for what's preoccupying their friends by taking a quick look at Facebook, for example, but they'll avoid getting bogged down in pointless online debates by stepping away from social media after just a few minutes.

Shannen, for example, practices minimalism in her online life. She juggles careers in writing and technology, and she's whip-smart, so in the medium of Twitter she's a natural. However, she deploys the 'block' and 'unfollow' button liberally. She believes Twitter can become a needlessly negative place that can affect people's mental health, and, as a busy mother and writer, she feels that she has enough on her plate. She also has an app that bars her access to social media beyond a set time in the late evening; it allows her to keep an eye on what's making the news without interrupting her time with her partner and child.

Shannen has found a way of making social media work for her: she can communicate with other professionals in her field, even if they live hundreds of miles away; she can promote her work and maintain a presence online; and she can dip a toe in the maelstrom of social media feeds when necessary.

For Shannen, real life – with her partner and child, her work, her friends – is happening offline, not in a small device that can be slipped into her handbag.

KICKING THE HABIT

So, how much of your time online is spent doing something of true value? To moving you closer to achieving any of your goals? And what are you avoiding by mindlessly snacking on social media?

Even if we admit that much of our social media activity isn't a good use of our time, using digital technology can be a tough habit to break. Anybody who has tried to stamp out a relatively harmless habit such as biting one's fingernails will be aware just how difficult it can be to put an end to a pattern of behavior. For years, we were told that it takes 21 days for a fresh routine to become a new habit. However, in 2009, psychology researcher Phillippa Lally published the results of a study that showed that it had taken an average of 66 days for participants to form a new habit.[55] (The study provides some comfort to those of us who every year struggle to adopt a bracing new gym habit by the third week of January.)

The best approach in trying to cut your social media usage is to use the technique of bringing friction into the habit you're trying to eliminate.

We saw in Chapter 2 how removing friction can make the working day run more smoothly. The opposite of this – inserting friction into a process – can make an action so unpalatable that it becomes impractical. Long before the dawn of social media, back when we relied on alarm clocks to wake us up rather than on our smartphones, I had a habit of sleeping through my radio alarm. To be more accurate, I had a habit of hitting the snooze button, then falling back to sleep. It was my boss who gave me the following tip: place the alarm clock on the opposite side of the room. This forced me to crawl out from under the covers when the alarm went off, and by the time I'd located the snooze button I'd be wide awake.

I was dubious, but the ploy worked. When the clock was beside my bed, turning off the irritating alarm was a smooth maneuver that caused me no discomfort; when the clock was moved beyond my reach, and I had to leave my bed to prevent the entire house being roused, the unpleasant sensation of leaving my cocoon-like bed jolted me out of my habitual action of dropping off again.

Today's app designers have devised equivalent solutions for people who are trying to unplug from the constant stream of social media posts. You can now choose from a wide range of apps that will block Facebook, Twitter, or Instagram for a set period.

HELP IS AT HAND

Sometimes we can help see off a bad habit by exchanging it for a good one. But first it's worth determining what need we're hoping to satisfy when we idly scroll through our social media. Are we seeking a momentary break from work, a slight reset of our thinking? Or are we feeling lonely and want a 'hit' of social media that will make us feel less isolated?

For instance, I know that when I'm sitting at my desk, writing, from time to time I need to take a minute away from the task in hand to gather my thoughts. That's typically when I find my eye wandering to my smartphone and my mind recalling that I posted a pithy little update earlier that just might have gained a little traction online. But what I really need is just a momentary break, so I make sure that I have a glass of water nearby. I can take a sip and achieve the same result, but it's a break that's over in the blink of an eye and one that's less likely to lead me down a rabbit hole of pointless celebrity gossip.

If you find your cue to check in on social media
is a brief pang of loneliness, harness that
feeling by sending a quick text to a friend.

Just let your friend know that you're thinking of them and hope to meet up soon. It will fulfill that need for social interaction without leading to the mindless overconsumption of insubstantial tweets or Facebook updates.

So instead of reaching for your smartphone whenever you feel slightly bored or in need of distraction, try to redirect that impulse toward something more useful and less likely to lead to further distractions, such as increasing your water consumption, or doing gentle stretches that will bring your attention back to the here and now.

Ultimately, just like every other bad habit, snapping out of a compulsion to regularly check your smartphone comes down to a matter of willpower. It means determining why you want to make a change to your habits, and following through on the action required on a consistent basis – however long it takes. It's true that it requires commitment, but think about how many good habits you already have, how consistent you are in your work and personal life. Making considered, intentional use of tweets or Instagram posts is simply another habit that you'll forge.

What makes new habits sustainable in the longer term is to come up with strategies that will help to reinforce them and help us adjust our mind-set. Technology is so integral to our lives that it would be difficult to exist in the modern world without it. So, even in instances where you've already taken steps to scale down your engagement with digital devices and social media, it may be necessary to reframe your relationship with technology on a more ongoing basis.

Again, ask yourself how you can be purposeful in the manner in which you use digital technology. Bear in mind that your response, and the actions you decide to take, will depend on your own circumstances and requirements.

Seven simple steps to cut back on social media

1. Take a regular day-long break from your devices

While I can see the appeal of taking a 30-day fast from my smartphone, in my case it isn't very practical. I live alone, and without the messaging services, social media portals, and the facility to make video calls that my smartphone gives me, I'd feel very isolated. So going cold turkey isn't an option for me – but I've taken steps toward cutting back by making a significant reduction on tech for one day a week, in my case on Sundays. In recent months I've committed to switching off the social media streams of

Facebook, Twitter, Instagram, and other online messaging boards for a 24-hour period, again during the weekend.

If it's practical to do so, take a day-long break from your devices and place them out of sight (though it's a good idea to increase the volume of your ringtone in case someone is trying to contact you). Sunday is a good day to pick, particularly if you don't observe a religious Sabbath. It restores the day to an occasion of rest and relaxation that will prepare you for the week ahead.

As you look at the role of digital technology and social media in your life, think about the extent to which it helps you either forge genuine connections with people or further your career – or whether it serves as a pointless distraction or fuels feelings of inadequacy. Perhaps a handful of elements of each platform serve a purpose and are worth keeping. For example, Facebook is where I'll find members of my extended family, or people I used to work with, so the messaging function on that platform is invaluable for keeping in touch. And if I want to find out what is trending, I'll dip into Twitter, where the pool of people I follow is 10 times larger.

So ask yourself what elements of social media are serving you well. Focus on those functions and phase out the features that have become a time sink.

2. Switch off notifications

Notifications are the distinctive little 'dings' that can spark either joy or anxiety – and do little more than impose themselves on your time. Notifications are useful if you're waiting for a specific message or if you work in a job where you're on call. But in the ordinary course of things, notifications serve only to lure you back to a certain social media platform or app. Turning notifications off is a simple maneuver, particularly when you remember that you can easily find out what's happening on social media by checking in at a time of your own choosing.

3. Make mealtimes phone-free

I'm as guilty as anybody of hovering over a restaurant table, angling for the perfect picture of whatever main course I've been served. But even I can concede that in recent years smartphones have become the uninvited guests when friends get together for a meal. So place your phone in your bag as soon as you arrive; or, if you're conscious that somebody may need to contact you, leave your phone face-down on the table with the voice call notification set to the buzzer.

When you're with family, set an example to children by not bringing your phone to the table at all.

4. Avoid bedside charging

It's tempting to make your final task before you go to sleep to quickly plug in your phone to recharge overnight. But its presence beside your bed can all too easily be the cue for you to start idly flicking through social media feeds. Ideally, you shouldn't bring smartphones or tablets into the bedroom at all. But if you use your smartphone as an alarm clock, or if you prefer the security of having your smartphone nearby, use an app that will block social media access; some still allow telephone calls, however.

5. Charge your phone in the hallway

As we settle down on the sofa after a busy day, it's too easy to plug in our smartphone beside us and keep checking social media when we should be spending quality time with loved ones or enjoying a good book. There's no need for you to have your smartphone on you 24/7 when you're in your own home. If you've decided to reduce your phone's role at home, let it live and charge largely in either the hallway or the kitchen — locations where you're usually immersed in other tasks, or there's high footfall. Reclaiming it for a browse of social media will then be a purposeful act, rather than something you do every five minutes just because it's in the pocket of your jeans. Again, if you're concerned about missing a call or text, adjust the settings so that these arrive with the appropriate ding.

6. Set limits at work

For most of us, technology has become an essential part of our working lives. But unless you're a coder or a computer programmer, work-based digital technology most likely remains a tool that's supposed to help you with your core role. However, it can be easy to forget this when you're faced with a teeming email inbox on a Monday morning and you feel the pressure to reply to every sender.

Tasks such as processing emails are better handled in batches, not on a piecemeal basis as they arrive in your inbox. So, choose two or three points during the day to check your email inbox and either reply, delete, or decide on a time to deal with the issue that's been raised. Turn off your email notifications on your desktop computer and feel how pleasant it is to read your email on your own terms, not those of a computer program.

7. Unplug from it all occasionally

Thanks to advances in digital technology, we have a world of entertainment at our fingertips. There are almost no circumstances today in which we can't access our favorite social media, our favorite music, a podcast or two.... We outlined above how boredom has become a forgotten concept and that, with the constant company of technology, we may be in danger of losing the facility to mull things over during a quiet walk in the countryside; to contemplate issues while weeding the garden. Our mobile technology means we need never feel alone, yet we often leave little room for spontaneous personal exchanges along the way. So take the time to unplug from it all occasionally. Reacquaint yourself with the sound of silence. Perhaps say hello to a stranger. See what happens.

....

As digital technology tightens its grip on our lives, we all have questions to ask about its scope and reach. Over the past decade or so, each one of us has negotiated our own terms for how we use social media, inevitably making errors along the way. And as technology develops, that process will inevitably continue apace. What's vitally important is that technology isn't allowed to interfere with the essence of who we truly are, nor hinder us as we pursue our goals.

In the end, when it comes to digital media, minimalism requires you to ask yourself:

- To what extent is technology helping me in the goals I've set for myself?

- What in my use of digital technology brings values to my life?

- How can I be more purposeful in my use of technology?

Once you've answered these questions, you'll be able to construct a set of priorities for your use of technology – a system that upholds your values and which will help you to achieve your goals.

CHAPTER 6

THE INSIDE JOB

You've cleared away the clutter in your wardrobes, you've become a purposeful, more engaged, and creative person at work, and you've stopped being a slave to your smartphone.

So perhaps it's time to take a look even closer to home? At yourself.

The minimalist lifestyle is a perfect fit for anybody who wants to go into the future with a genuine pep in their step. Its focus on pared-down simplicity is much like current medical wisdom – that a diet of simple, nutritious food, and following a simple lifestyle, will yield considerable health benefits in the long run. Meanwhile, if minimalism is about bringing intentionality into your life, are you being intentional in relation to your health? Are you applying the same discipline and vigor to your eating habits and exercise regime that you applied to putting the basement in order? And where does mental health fit in?

One of the most beautiful places I've ever visited is the Nicoya peninsula on Costa Rica's west coast. Its beaches attract surfers from around the world, while agriculture thrives in its verdant landscapes, and its towns and villages hum with activity. It also happens to be a Blue Zone, a region identified by Dan Buettner, a fellow of the National Geographic Society, as a place where locals are more likely to live to 100.[56] Buettner has written extensively about how certain pockets of the world – certain mountain villages in Sardinia, Italy; the islands of Okinawa, Japan; the tiny city of Loma Linda in California; the Greek island of Ikaria; and Nicoya – are sites of extraordinary feats of longevity. According to one 2013 study, the average 60-year-old Nicoya man is almost seven times more likely to reach his 100th birthday than his Japanese counterpart.[57]

For Buettner, who has made a study of life in these regions, they have a number of factors in common: people have a strong sense of purpose; they benefit from strong social and family bonds; they practice religion, or another form of spirituality; their stress levels are quite low; they enjoy a moderate intake of alcohol; they take regular moderate exercise; and their calorie intake stays within the 'moderate' range – that is, they tend not to eat to excess.

For thousands of years, the human body has been a site of wonder for poets and healers, scribes and apothecaries. For every step forward that science makes in throwing light onto its mysteries, the body reveals another layer of opacity and complexity that inspires only awe. Certainly, nobody who has borne witness to a child's first faltering steps, watched their personality emerge before they've uttered their first words, or seen the beauty in an elderly woman's face, could fail to be enchanted at the human condition.

THE EFFECT OF OUR MODERN LIFESTYLE

But at some point over the past hundred years or so, our bodies became the site of a science experiment. Many of the foods we'd consumed for thousands of years suddenly became off-limits, and the natural shape of our bodies became unacceptable. Modern work practices, the popularity of the motor car, and the new, sprawling nature of our towns and cities all began working against lifestyles that had helped us burn off calories over the course of the day.

Just two or three generations ago,
people thrived on simple diets.

For the most part, the two or three meals they enjoyed each day were made from ingredients that had come from the surrounding area. In the case of my grandparents, living in rural Ireland, the most exotic item on the daily menu would have been the loose-leaf tea they drank with every meal. Nearly everything else would have come from either the family farm – say, potatoes, cabbage, and bacon – or from the local shop, which supplied only plain food, such as large sacks of flour or 2lb bags of sugar (which came from the sugar-processing plant about 20 miles away that bought sugar beet from my grandfather's farm). There was a neat air of self-sufficiency about the lifestyle. Meanwhile, their lives of labor-intensive farm work and a home life devoid of modern appliances meant that the calories they consumed were more or less expended over the course of the working day.

Fast-forward to today, when entire aisles of the supermarket are given over to snack foods that have little nutritional value but will boost calorie intake for the consumer. A recent glance at my local major supermarket is revelatory. While shoppers can help themselves to thousands of lines of products with delicious ingredients hailing from every corner of the globe and drawing on the world's most tantalizing cuisines, the biggest display is given over to potato chips, cookies, and candy. It's depressing.

What's even more depressing, for me, is recalling those occasions when I've feasted on entire packets of chips but barely registered them as a savory event. I still remember a particular low point. It was a night I'd been looking forward to for months: my favorite Sunday-night TV drama was returning after the summer hiatus, and I'd read enough hype to know that tonight's episode was going to be a classic; a water-cooler moment that we'd be talking about for weeks, if not months, to come. To mark the occasion, I made plans to watch the show alone and bought a bottle of wine. I even prepared – in a selection of ramekins – an array of chips, fries, salsa, salted crackers, and cheese. I set out the various dishes, with their little portions of treats, on a tray that I'd set with a checkered tea cloth. Completing the look was the large glass of white wine. It seemed like an appropriate way to mark the end of the weekend and to welcome back my favorite characters.

So it was with no little satisfaction that I set the tray down on the coffee table and sat back to enjoy Episode 1 of the show. The credits rolled, I sat back, and rested the glass of wine on the armrest beside me. About 20 minutes later, I reached for another small handful of chips and found... an empty bowl. That bowl had been full just five minutes before the start of the program. What had happened? I switched on the light beside me but this only confirmed the situation: I'd managed to scarf down all of the chips and make indecent inroads into the fries and salsa. The cheese was surviving quite well but I'd lost my appetite. I could barely remember eating any of the chips after the initial satisfying crunch accompanying the first frame of the TV drama. Within the space of about 20 minutes, I'd eaten probably a few hundred calories without even noticing. I'd gone to the trouble of making these few treats into a little picnic for myself, and all the pleasure of eating it had completely passed me by. I could have wept with frustration!

The truth is, there have been many occasions over the years where I've absentmindedly picked at food that was neither tasty nor nutritionally beneficial. Cheese-and-wine receptions, fancy canapés at holiday-season soirées, pizzas that my bosses stumped up for on high-pressure work nights. As a reporter, I must have attended hundreds of events where the hosts had laid on delicious hors d'oeuvres and on-trend delicacies, yet although I remember platters of food, and perfecting my party piece of juggling a wine glass, appetizer, and notebook, I don't think any of these tasters stand out as a properly culinary experience.

Yet food is one of life's great pleasures. Many people devote their lives to bringing out the very best qualities in their raw ingredients to serve up to an appreciative public, while others devote their lives to tracking down and sampling for themselves the purest expression of a chef's art. Meanwhile, campaigners such as food writer Jack Monroe have, in the face of great income inequality, advocated strongly for food to be stripped of its elitist symbolism and be restored to its place at the heart of the family, as a source of sustenance, both nutritionally and emotionally.

THE IMPACT OF MARKETING

At its most basic, food is fuel. It's true that a meal shared with friends and family seems to taste that little bit better than any solo feast, and in a social setting food can play a tremendous role in bringing people together, helping people to create memories, and passing on family values and traditions to the next generation. But fundamentally, food is a form of sustenance that's supposed to nourish us physically. In itself, food isn't supposed to entertain us, or cheer us on, or take the place of a good cry after our heart has been broken.

And it certainly isn't designed to be a side dish – literally – to a TV drama, which was the mistake I made. Eating snack food from time to time is inevitable – perhaps even pleasing as a treat from time to time. But wolfing down handfuls of potato chips and sweets without even realizing is having the worst of both worlds: you consume hundreds of calories without properly appreciating the tastes and textures you've been indulging in.

Even worse, clever marketing drives much snack-food consumption. Just think about the last time you bought a treat for yourself from a convenience store. What was it, and why did you choose it? Was it because it's an old favorite – and why is it an old favorite? Is it because the combination of slightly pallid chocolate and artificial flavorings is simply irresistible? Or is it a favorite because, well, you've been buying it for years, probably since the days of your childhood when it was regarded as a rare treat, and you remember when the TV commercial featured some of your favorite cartoon characters...?

In fact, your purchasing decision will have been made on the basis of many factors: the positioning of that chocolate bar in the convenience store, decades of brand marketing, your fondness for a bar you associate with your childhood, your own mood on the day...

When it comes down to it, whether you were hungry may not have been relevant at all.

It's why billions of dollars are spent every year in making sure that the world's biggest brand names remain visible on our TVs, in our magazines, on our smartphones (it's been estimated that people see some 5,000 marketing images every day). Some brands even manage to become part of the cultural landscape, with their products lodged in the collective imagination. It's part of the reason I refuse to berate myself for the times that my eyes fix on a popular soda on the menu when I'm asked in a restaurant what I'd like to drink.

There's no turning back the clock to a time before the food and advertising industries infiltrated our consciences. But simply being aware of the external forces that are trying to marshal you into making certain consumer choices goes a long way toward discerning what exactly you want. Practicing the principles of minimalism, and focusing on living an intentional life, helps us to tune out many of the commercially driven messages we see every day and to concentrate on our true wants and needs. To counter the bombardment of messages from powerful commercial interests urging us to buy, buy, buy, sometimes we need to bring a little intentionality to our internal forces.

BRING INTENTION TO YOUR EATING HABITS

When was the last time you helped yourself to something from the cookie jar, and why? Did you indulge because you truly felt a need for it? Were you down in the dumps? Or were you bored, or feeling listless?

Were you even hungry?

The next time you feel the need to reach for the cookie jar or order takeout via a smartphone app, ask yourself: *Am I hungry – or am I just bored, listless, down in the dumps, or lonely? If I'm not hungry, will eating this snack really make a difference to my state? Or will I end up feeling bloated yet somehow not truly satisfied? Would a better use of my time be to read a book or watch my favorite Netflix show? Would I be better off phoning or Skyping a friend or family member for a catch-up? Or shall I simply delete the meal-delivery app from my smartphone....*

Of course, bringing intention to our eating
habits extends beyond snack time.

It starts before you even hit the supermarket. I've found over the years that the easiest way of avoiding situations where I'm mindlessly reaching for a junk food snack is by doing a little menu planning – and making sure that I'm never too far from a nutritious meal.

That means I'll have either had a nutritious meal in the previous four or five hours, or I'll make sure that there's a nutritious meal coming soon. If I'm at home, I'll have all the ingredients for a nutritious meal on hand; it may not be a slap-up three-course meal, but in a tight squeeze I can rustle up a pretty mean broccoli and anchovy pasta dish out of a handful of pantry items and some fresh broccoli. With a little more advance planning, I can plan the week's menus as I formulate my shopping list, and try to be a little more creative with what's in season.

The real pleasure, of course, is in eating. It's taken a few years but I think I've finally come to appreciate good food – that is, food that's been made from excellent ingredients and which has been prepared with care.

SLOW IT DOWN

Whatever is on your plate, the first step is to pause before you dive into the dish. We eat with our eyes, as chefs are told during their rigorous apprenticeship. That advice captures the extent to which we're sensory creatures – how our sense of taste can be enhanced by a tantalizing sight or mouthwatering scent. Note the various colors and shapes, and the different textures, of the food in front of you, and the various smells.

Once you're ready to raise you fork, take your time. Take a bite and consider the texture and the taste. Notice how the textures of the various elements on the plate intermingle, how the sensation changes as you chew, and whether you're aware of other tastes away from the dominant ingredient. Chew slowly and deliberately.

After the first 10 or so mouthfuls, put your fork down for a few minutes before resuming.

Eating slowly helps the process by which the brain can register when the stomach is full. When you feel full, simply stop eating, and relax.

Even if all I'm eating is my very simple dish of *al dente* broccoli and pasta, dressed in warm olive oil that's been infused with anchovy, garlic, and chopped chili, I find there's a world of taste and texture to enjoy. In visual terms, the vivid green of the broccoli florets contrasts with the cream color of the pasta, with little darts of black pepper seasoning. With the first forkful, I'll be hit with the heat of the chili as I crunch on the still-firm broccoli, and the oil-coated pasta gives a satisfying contrast with every bite. After a second or so, however, the pungent garlic and the salty anchovy supersede the chili. With every mouthful offering up a variation on these tastes and textures, this unfussy pasta dish makes a feast – and all because I take my time to truly savor all the elements.

Minimalism often comes in for criticism over perceptions that it's a harsh, ascetic regimen that brings little joy. But food prepared with care from the best ingredients one can lay one's hands on represents one of the greatest expressions of mankind's talents. And the principles of minimalism provide a focus to enjoy the essential qualities of food. They bring to bear a certain intentionality about what one chooses to eat, whether it's a feast by a Michelin-starred chef or a humble plate of pasta.

Ultimately, the point of minimalism isn't to demonize particular types of food. Most people find that they function better when they minimize the role of junk food in their diet, or they moderate their alcohol intake.

Minimalism is about letting adults make informed decisions about how they treat their own body.

It's about listening to your body's needs and basing your choices on how best you can supply the nutrients it needs.

If your body occasionally cries out for a couple of brownies, they can be accommodated by the principles of minimalism as long as you remain true to your answer to the question: 'What value does this bring?'

EXERCISE TO REVITALIZE

It was one of the most bruising experiences of my life: I was the assistant editor on a glossy magazine but, along with my colleagues, I'd been laid off from my job. It meant that 75 percent of my income would disappear overnight. Meanwhile, I was single, I had a mortgage, and I was working in a dying industry: the newspaper trade. The outlook wasn't good: I depended on routine to keep me on an even keel, and I'd long since recognized that I over-identified with my glamorous-sounding job. Eventually, thanks to the support of friends I'd made over the years, I picked up other work, but for a few long weeks I felt shaken, and one of the few things that got me over the hump was a new habit I was beginning to hone. Just weeks before the bosses had pulled the plug on my job, I'd embarked on a 'Couch to 5K' program. I wasn't about to break any speed records, but I enjoyed the sense of achievement I felt when I completed each step of the regime, and I liked the slight tingle of strain in my muscles when I completed a run. Through so many of the dark days when I wondered where my future lay, I knew I could count on one certainty: that my legs would be able to carry me along the jogging path near my home, and that the effort wouldn't kill me!

As someone who had avoided exercise for most of their life (through a cunning manipulation of my timetable, I managed to skip PE for the final two years of school), it was the first time I'd experienced for myself the magical effects of exercise. And all I needed to achieve it was a pair of good trainers.

We've long known about the health benefits of exercise: it helps with anxiety; it leads to the release of endorphins (the hormones associated with happiness); it can help with weight loss; it leaves us feeling energized – but all too often it can feel like we don't have time to hit the gym or sign up for that spin class.

Most health experts would agree that finding the time for exercise is essential. It's not an optional extra in our lifestyle. The World Health Organization (WHO) recommends that adults aged 18–64 get 75 minutes of vigorous intensity exercise every week.[58] After all, depending on the form it takes, exercise can improve cardiovascular function, improve bone strength, undo many of the effects of aging, improve one's self-confidence, help brain health and memory, and lead to the building of social connections.

And the best news is that exercise pays dividends even at entry-level. If you're starting from a low base, simple measures like committing to a 20-minute walk two or three times a week can make a big difference to your overall fitness and physical well-being.

So why is it so difficult to reach for the running shoes? Why do we end up vegging out on the sofa instead of hitting the gym? Why do we talk ourselves out of going for that walk?

All too often, the thought of taking part in any form of physical exertion just seems too much after a hectic day at work. But if minimalism is about focusing on what's important, shouldn't your physical fitness be at the very heart of that?

If your health is your wealth, then taking care of your body should be something that you schedule into your week.

As with so many things in life, finding the time is about setting your priorities.

Ultimately, sticking to a commitment to take exercise two or three times a week means making a determined effort. Perhaps it'll mean diverting time away from something else – but working out is one of the best uses of your time. After all, you're quite literally investing in yourself.

READY, STEADY, GO

Find a way of incorporating exercise into your day. Perhaps due to childcare commitments, or long commuting times, it suits you to go to the gym at lunchtime instead of before or after work. Sure, you'll miss the catch-up with your colleagues, but if you can enlist a friend for your workout you can still turn it into a social occasion. Personally, I can't bear working out in the evening; the gym is too crowded, and there are queues for the equipment. Nor do I like exercising on a full stomach. So I time my workouts to take place either before breakfast, since I have the flexibility of working from home, or before lunch. Figure out what works for you, in terms of your own preferences and in relation to your circumstances.

It helps to find a form of exercise that you enjoy, and to mix things up from time to time. For some people, the gym is the stuff of nightmares: an enclosed space with too many mirrors and too many people flexing for the 'gram. Perhaps you prefer being out in the fresh air and would feel more at home joining a 'Couch to 5K' 'beginners' group. Or perhaps you could sign up for one aerobics class and spend two lunchtimes during the week taking a brisk walk in the park near your office.

The WHO guidelines of 75 minutes of vigorous exercise every week – that's three 25-minute sessions of physical activity – is an excellent goal to have in your sights. As you adjust to the new regimen, you may find that you need a fresh challenge, so investigate other options that might fit into your week. When I worked in an office on the other side of town from my home, I had a routine of jogging for 30 minutes on three days of the week, and cycling to and from work (about 6 miles away) once or twice a week; my cycling was even less vigorous than my jogging but it served the purpose of ticking the box of 'physical activity,' as well as getting me out into the fresh air, and being enjoyable.

MAKE HABITS THAT LAST

As with so many habits, a creative approach to removing friction can be helpful here. Friction is a set of conditions that make an action that little bit harder to contemplate.

When we're trying to adopt a new habit, we should aim to make the experience as frictionless as possible by removing as many barriers as we can.

When I completed the 'Couch to 5K' and wanted to maintain the habit, I'd place my running gear on the bed before going to sleep: it meant that when I woke up the following morning, I didn't have to look for, say, a pair of running socks before going for my workout.

More than anything, however, the best way of sticking with a new habit is by basing it not on the process (say, running) or even the outcome (a fitter, perhaps trimmer, body) but by doing a little rewiring. According to James Clear, the author of *Atomic Habits*,[59] the most effective way to forge a new habit is to decide to incorporate the characteristics of the new practice into your identity, something I found out for myself, both in my own experience of running and in the people I met along the way. The people who managed to maintain the discipline and routine of training after the initial honeymoon period (and we saw earlier that it can take hundreds of days for a new behavior to become habit[60]) would refer to themselves as 'runners.'

If you want to embark on an exercise regimen, what goal do you have in mind? Do you want to be a person who goes to the gym three nights a week? Do you ultimately want to be a person who runs a marathon? Do you want to be a person who isn't exhausted after playing with their children for 30 minutes?

Whatever your goal is, what would your life look like if you were to attain it? How would it feel to have that level of fitness? Quietly at first – because in time, the entire world will know – say to yourself, 'I'm that person: I'm somebody who goes to the gym three nights a week... I'm somebody who runs marathons... I'm somebody who relishes running around with the children....' Now take the first step toward making that vision a reality. Book a session with the personal trainer at your local gym, print off a copy of a 'Couch to 5K' schedule, plan a 30-minute walk for this evening. With time, and commitment, of course, you'll find that you'll steadily make gains on achieving your goal.

But perhaps you feel that you've simply missed the boat on physical fitness; that seeing as you didn't engage with it when you were in school or in your early twenties, there's little point now. But if the best time to plant a tree was 20 years ago, the second best time is now. And if the best time to take up exercise was when you were in high school, or when you were young and moderately fit, the second best time is also now.

MENTAL HEALTH MATTERS

After decades of being largely ignored and treated as a taboo, mental health is finally getting its day in the sun. There's greater acceptance that our mental health is a precious resource that must be nurtured and cared for. As well-known figures open up about their struggles with mental health, more and more of us are educating ourselves in how we can cultivate habits that will give regular top-ups to our mental health.

Minimalism, applied to our lives on an ongoing basis, helps clear the decks for us so that we can enjoy more time with the people we love.

Of course, if you're clinically depressed or have clinical anxiety, your first port of call should be your family doctor. However, minimalist principles can help you identify what is most important, and let you live the life you truly want to lead.

One of the ways in which minimalism has helped me shore up my mental health is the sense of agency, of being able to do something about my circumstances. Life has a habit of throwing curveballs – redundancy, illness, bereavement – but by living with intentionality and exerting control over what material items come into my home, I feel like I'm retaining some control right at the heart of where I spend most of my time. In a world where we can control very little, that's a powerful act. After all, one cornerstone of good mental health is feeling secure and happy in one's home, no matter how big or small.

Our homes provide us with a sense of sanctuary.

Home is where we go when we want to recharge after a day's work or we simply want to close the door on the hurly-burly of everyday life.

For some of us, a minimalist home nourishes our inner well-being by being a quiet, uncluttered space of visual calm where we collect our thoughts before heading out into the world once more. I rather like this model of the minimalist home. Unfortunately, it doesn't chime with the more worn version of reality that I (and most of my friends) live in, where photographs of my family take precedence over any aesthetic. But this is what I like about minimalism: it's not about sticking rigidly to a set of rules that can make us miserable; it's not about getting the number of possessions we own down to a set figure. It's about living with intentionality, being at peace with our surroundings, and applying simplicity to our lives in a way that leaves room for what really matters.

> A minimalist lifestyle offers us the opportunity
> to practice 'mindfulness of things.'

We can sit or stand in the middle of our living space and, as we look around, we know that every item is either an object of beauty, plays a vital role in our everyday lives, or represents a precious memory or a facet of our life that we hold dear. We can also teach our children about mindfulness and the importance of being in the moment. Although we may slip up from time to time, our home represents the essence of who we are, and we can feel comfortable. It's a place where we can be ourselves, and where maintaining our surroundings is a manageable task, not an endless series of chores.

However, if striving for a minimalist lifestyle is causing you distress, step back. Just as minimalism isn't about getting the number of your possessions down to a magic number, neither is it about clearing your home of your most precious memories. If you find decluttering upsetting, with no sense of freedom or clarity of mind, simply take a break.

MAKE YOUR HOME YOUR SANCTUARY

Living in a minimalist space should be liberating. I like the fact that my surroundings are calming, that my progress around my little flat is unimpeded by clutter. For many of us, clutter –

mounds of papers, CDs no one listens to, electronic devices that no longer work – have an oppressive effect on us. The sight of them reminds us of bills that have to be filed, dusting that we failed to do, and poorly thought-out purchasing decisions. Living with clutter is dispiriting and drains us of mental energy. Its presence in our living environment, in our workspace, even on our computer tablets, means that it's difficult to find the things we need.

Implementing a healthy declutter from time to time helps us to feel that we're taking back control over our possessions. Of course you'll feel an attachment to the teacup and saucer from Granny's kitchen long ago, but don't let that same warm feeling extend, say, to the mass-produced travel coffee cup that a friend brought home as a souvenir from Florida a couple of years ago.

For some people, just the thought of a declutter, of having to make a tough call on what mementos from the past will have to hit the dumpster, is a source of stress. But remember that for every item of great sentimental value, there will be 10 pieces of commercial junk you've accumulated over the years.

Once you have a firm fix on what's worth hanging on to, it'll be easy to dispose of the worthless stuff that serves no purpose.

And looking forward, simply taking stock of your possessions from time to time, and throwing out dated odds and ends, goes a long way toward making decluttering jobs less intimidating.

If clutter can induce stress, one obvious solution is simply to stop it from coming into your home in the first place. As I've negotiated my own life within minimalism, I've found myself spending less and less time in shops and boutiques idly looking for something, anything, to buy. These days, if I have to go into a large store, I usually find it overwhelming, so I'll stick in my earphones and listen to a podcast or some calming music while I search for what I need. But 21st-century consumerism is a powerful force. So rampant is its desire to shift stock that manufacturers no longer depend on bricks-and-mortar shops to sell their wares, and opportunities to splash the cash now come via the smartphone you carry with you everywhere.

Another consequence of the cash splurges (whether online or at your local mall) may well be your credit card balance inching upward, causing increasing pressure on your finances that may have a harmful effect on your mental health. According to the Royal College of Psychiatrists, debt is a cause of many mental health problems.[61]

Even if you're in a financial position where debt isn't a pressing concern, there's evidence that pursuing a lifestyle that prioritizes material gain instead of valuing relationships or personal development can make for a miserable life. Earlier we noted that psychology professor Tim Kasser reported that 'the more highly people endorsed materialistic values, the more they experienced unpleasant emotions, depression and anxiety... the less they experienced pleasant emotions and felt satisfied with their lives.' He speculated that people who lead more materialistic lifestyles find that their 'psychological needs to feel free, competent and connected to other people' went unmet.[62]

It's been said that this generation is in the grip of a 'loneliness epidemic';[63] that two in five Americans (43 percent) 'sometimes or always feel that their relationships are not meaningful' and report feeling isolated from others.[64]

It's true that minimalism calls on us to direct our gaze inward to a certain extent, but the principles of minimalism are also designed to enable us to have the best life we can; to minimize the psychological space given over to pursuing the acquisition of material possessions; to make room for people instead of things; and to make it easier to reach out and establish relationships of warmth and authenticity.

Think minimalist, maximize your mental health

One of the first things everybody remarks on after they've embarked on a declutter is the liberating sensation of newly cleared space in their home. So let your thoughts reflect your new surroundings, your new work habits, your new relationships. Let your thoughts be as clear and as uncluttered as the environment you've created for yourself.

1. Live in the present

You're sitting on a beach, soaking up the last few rays of the sun as you watch it set. But you can't enjoy it. There's work tomorrow, and the project you have to finish off, and the fact that the washing machine is on its last legs.... It's an all too frequent occurrence: the intrusion of an uncertain future into the here and now – and when the present isn't as idyllic as glorying in a magnificent sunset. Many of us find ourselves shuttling between the future and the past as we negotiate our daily lives. Sometimes it's your present self trying to be mindful of your future self – in which case, make a note and let the impulse drift away from your consciousness. But sometimes it's the replaying of scenes from our past, the re-enactment of our worst mistakes, which assails us out of the blue. As a logical person, you know what's past is past, and that whatever happened, you've learnt your lesson from it. Take a deep breath and try to return to the here and now, to a point in time where you can actually control events and start forming a better future.

2. Complain less

It's good to vent from time to time – necessary, even – but complaining can easily become a deeply ingrained habit, and one that's hard to break. And sometimes, endlessly discussing our dismay has the effect of making the issue loom larger in our lives than it should. What's worse is that very often complaining is so exhausting that the perpetrator can't find the energy to change what's annoying them. If you find that you seem to keep circling back to the same topic of how certain situations or people irritate you, just stop and ask yourself a few questions. Has complaining resolved the situation so far? What can you do to remove yourself from the situation of being annoyed? If you must put up with it, how can you reconcile yourself to it being part of your life for the foreseeable future? Take back some of the power in this situation by working out how to manage your irritation. It's too easy for dissatisfaction in one area of our lives to spread to other elements of it, making us miserable overall. Nip the worry in the bud by either resolving the situation, or changing your response to it.

3. Celebrate your achievements

We're inclined to beat ourselves up over the feats we haven't managed to achieve. But don't forget to pat yourself on the back for the things you succeeded at. If you've cleared the garage of years of clutter, give yourself a mental high-five! If you've used the same clarity of purpose to define your goals, well done! If you've started a new exercise regimen, congratulations! These are all vital steps toward creating the future you deserve. Even better, they represent the progress you made since your home was awash with junk, you were listlessly drifting through life, and you hadn't the motivation to get up from your couch.

It's true that in order to see real results, you'll have to put in the effort and maintain momentum in the weeks and months to come, but you're laying solid foundations for the future. Meanwhile, try not to compare your life, your milestones, your social media analytics with others' lives online, or with some fantasy version of yourself. Comparison really is the thief of joy, and serves no useful purpose other than draining away our sense of initiative and wasting our time. Put an end to it straight away.

4. Stop criticizing

Criticizing is slightly different from complaining. While the focus of complaining is usually the person doing the complaining, who typically feels wronged, criticism usually details the faults of another person or situation. But just like complaining, it can develop into a habit. You may believe you're a perceptive observer of character, but are you just the office harridan, somebody everybody tiptoes around? Do you offer penetrating insights into a family member's parenting techniques, or are you guilty of weighing in on a situation you know little about? Is your analysis of a friend's relationship history no more than delivering a few home truths, or is it a distasteful rehashing of a friend's vulnerabilities.

As with complaining, if you feel strongly about an issue, do something about it – either by helping out or by finding an expert in the relevant field who can help. Even more toxic is the habit of incessantly criticizing oneself for one's failings. We all have a harsh inner critic and most of the time our inner critic keeps us on the straight and narrow, flagging up potential dangers on the road ahead. But sometimes our inner critic is a little too robust with their chiding. Remember that your inner critic is just an aspect of your own personality. If the nagging becomes too much, throw yourself into a physical activity or go for a coffee with a friend. Just find a way to take a break from your own internal monologue of negativity!

5. Practice gratitude

How often do you count your blessings? Every morning, when I step into the shower, I give thanks for being born in the late 20th century. I can't help thinking how the sensation of hot needles of water landing on my skin, with its promise of effortless cleanliness, would have been unimaginable to my great-grandmother, who was born in the 19th century. It's only a small thing but it grounds me in the present while reminding me of my heritage, and how far we've come as a society. Once you start giving thanks for things, your eyes open to all sorts of wonders: a good novel, autumn leaves, being able to fit into your old jeans…. These pleasures may seem mundane but they can restore our sense of awe of the world and remind us of the abundance that surrounds us.

One last tip: Every day, do one thing that makes you happy, whether it's catching a glimpse of your favorite street from the upper deck of your bus to work, grabbing a coffee in your favorite café, or calling a friend for a catch-up. Celebrate the life you have – and the life you're preparing for.

....

'The mind is everything,' Buddha taught his disciples. 'What you think, you become.' Our thoughts have a power that doesn't always seem apparent to us. Certainly, not everybody who thinks about becoming an Olympic figure-skating champion ends up claiming a gold medal. But our impulses have a habit, when repeated often enough, of bedding down in the crevices of our minds, taking root and growing into long-lasting convictions that will shape many decisions in the years ahead. And unfortunately that includes our negative ones. According to research, humans have an average of 60,000 thoughts per day, many of them repetitive. If what we think is what we become, don't we owe it to ourselves to do away with negative, unproductive thoughts that may be cluttering our thinking? What's wonderful is that this step requires no special training or equipment: all that's needed is a commitment to boost the number of positive, encouraging thoughts that you formulate every day. It couldn't be simpler.

In all areas of health, whether it's your diet, your exercise regimen or the internal monologue that keeps you company all day long, make time to ask yourself: *How does this action, this thought, help me achieve my goals? Does this action, or this thought, bring value to my life?* If a habit or a thought process has no role to play in your pursuit of what you really want in life, if it's wasting valuable time and energy, it must be discarded and replaced by a practice that's more positive and which will lead to productive change.

More than any other resource, our health
must be protected and nurtured.

Without good health, it'll be virtually impossible to enjoy any of the delights that life has to offer, so it pays to be purposeful as you consider which foods you use to fuel your body, as well as the thoughts you use to fuel your mind, and how you utilize the remarkable machine that is the human body.

'If anything is sacred, the human body is sacred,' poet Walt Whitman once wrote.[65] Consider for a moment everything that your body does for you: breathing, eating, walking, running, copulating, giving birth.... Now, doesn't your body deserve the best shot at a healthy future? Don't you?

CONCLUSION

I sometimes wonder, will I ever be a good minimalist? Will I ever attain the level of restrained nirvana I see depicted whenever minimalism is discussed on TV or online? When I look at my eclectic collection of tea mugs, the mismatched towels on display in my bathroom, the cabbage-rose-print blouse that snuck into my wardrobe in recent years (and which I adore), it can feel as if I'm failing at minimalism.

As a 44-year-old woman with a soft spot for large-print fabrics, I may not fit the bill of what a typical minimalist looks like, but I can honestly say that the principles of minimalism have served me well. I no longer loiter on fashion websites, pouncing on 'bargain' dresses that turn out to have just six or seven wears in them; I can breeze past mobile phone shops without longing to road test the latest smartphone; and I can dip into social media without feeling slightly sullied by the experience.

As someone who has had a love-hate relationship with money for much of her adult life, I finally understand writer G.K. Chesterton's observation, 'There are two ways to get enough. One is to continue to accumulate more and more. The other is to desire less.'

I know that when I had wardrobes stuffed full with fashionable clothes, with my pick of cute outfits to wear to work every day, I was no happier than when, years later, my circumstances changed and I had to knock my shopping habit on the head. Living as we do in extraordinary times, more and more people are giving serious consideration to the concept of 'enough': why it's so difficult to attain, and whether the Earth should pay the price so that we can have 'enough' smartphones, tablets, and cars. Since discovering how I can bring minimalism into my life, I find that the clothes I already have are 'enough,' my two-year-old smartphone is 'enough,' my life – with or without the filtering feature of the latest social media app – is 'enough.'

Minimalism has also given me a fresh perspective, and a way of reclaiming some head space for myself in a world where the mountains of 'stuff' – useless junk in our homes, data-hungry apps on our smartphones, never-ending lists of work commitments – can feel overwhelming. Applying the principles of minimalism in the key areas of my life that are within my control – my home, my relationships, my work, my online life, my health – all help me feel on top of things, and that I have a certain amount of mastery over my fate.

I've lost count of the number of people who've quietly confessed, 'Minimalism? I'd love to try that – but I simply couldn't....' They say they wouldn't know where to start with decluttering their home. Or they have a growing family and they would never be able to enlist their partner and children. Or it just seems completely unattainable for the ordinary man or woman in their suburban, semi-detached home.

But minimalism is a practice that anybody can engage with. Although in the public mind it's associated with sleek, modern design, true minimalism doesn't require you to stick to a particular look or aesthetic. But it does call for rigorous discipline in asking certain questions of yourself as you go through life. It requires a high level of honesty and a commitment to being accountable to your own standards and values. Fundamentally, it puts the onus on you to set your own path in life by setting your own goals and working assiduously toward them. Along the way, you must decide what brings value to your life and what will help you progress toward your goals. Having determined what's important and truly serves you, you can simply discard the rest.

MINIMALISM IN PRACTICE

If these actions seem extreme, it's because too many of us have got used to having our wishes and dreams set aside, or pushed down other people's agendas. It's time to turn those wishes and dreams into goals – goals that you can achieve with willpower and determination.

AT HOME

By now, you'll have experienced the liberating feeling of decluttering your home and seeing your living space becoming lighter and brighter as a result. But it's vitally important that you maintain a routine of keeping shelves, wardrobes, and kitchen drawers free of extraneous stuff. Be strict with yourself and other members of the household: nothing new can come into the house unless it's really needed.

AT WORK

On the work front, you'll now have formulated a plan for attaining your professional goal and have embarked on the first few steps toward reaching it. Practice being purposeful with your time and energy, and streamline your working day so that you need not be distracted from what's absolutely essential.

WITH MONEY

As you spend some of your hard-earned cash, remember that money should work for you. If buying an item doesn't affect your long-term happiness and has no functional purpose, why are you buying it? Even if your goals in life are non-financial, try to secure a sound financial footing for your future self by saving regularly. Try also to frame your next purchase in terms of your time: you earned the money by exchanging your time and labor for your salary, so work out its value to you as an expression of hours of your life.

IN YOUR RELATIONSHIPS

Examine the relationships you have in your life – can you say that each relationship has an overall positive effect on your life? Sometimes friendships simply fizzle out, or curdle into something more toxic. Realize that your past doesn't have to define your future; there's a whole world of potential friends out there. All it takes to establish a bond is to harbor an openness of spirit and the willingness to take a chance by saying hello.

ON SOCIAL MEDIA

Offering us hundreds, if not thousands, of friends (or 'followers'), social media has turned our lives upside down. But although Twitter, Instagram, and Facebook can help us maintain friendships where there's a genuine connection, it's all too easy for the glossy nature of the medium to end up fostering resentment as we compare our own lives with the edited highlights of somebody else's heavily curated version of reality. Worse still, it can distract us from work or keep us cocooned from real life and real relationships. Return digital technology to its original role in your life: a tool that's supposed to work for you.

WITH YOUR HEALTH

If our health is our wealth, isn't it worth investing in your long-term physical and emotional well-being with the right diet and exercise? Instead of mindless grazing on snacks, try to take a mindful approach to eating, treating a nutritional weekday dinner in the same manner you would a five-course feast.

Find a way to incorporate exercise into your life in as seamless a manner as possible. Remember that 'what you think, you become,' so work on reducing the number of negative, toxic thoughts that cross your mind.

NEW LIFESTYLE, NEW YOU

By now, you may well have implemented a range of new habits across a broad sweep of your life. If those habits are 'sticking,' congratulations! If, on the other hand, some of your new habits are falling by the wayside, take heart: remember Phillippa Lally's research on habit formation, outlined in Chapter 5? She found that in a study of 96 people who were asked to add a new, healthier habit to their routine (healthy eating or drinking, or a new exercise habit), new habits were forged over a period that ranged from 18 to 254 days, with 66 the average number of days it took to adapt.[66]

The same research showed that the process of forming a new habit isn't as linear as you might think: there are often missteps along the way, as participants in the study found, but those instances of 'falling off the wagon' apparently had little impact on whether a new habit became a lasting routine. The research shows that if you've been broadly diligent about maintaining the new routine, and you make an effort to get back to it, there's a good chance that you'll reach the point where your new habit is an impulse that you act on automatically.

What's crucial is that you don't berate yourself for your mistakes and simply give up your new resolution as a pointless exercise. Dismantling one habit and putting a new one in its place can be exhausting. It's tiring to go from simply sitting in your car every morning to drive to work, to taking the bus or train instead. It's tiring to start cooking meals from scratch when preprepared salads have been your primary diet.

So you ordered takeout at the end of your first week of trying to make all your meals from scratch. Sure, it's not ideal, but look at it this way: how many meals did you prepare yourself this week compared with the week before? A substantially larger number, right? Tomorrow is another day, and by early next week you'll be back on track.

Be kind to yourself. As the weeks go by, you should find that the process will become smoother, and you may discover little 'hacks' that will make your new habit easier to incorporate into your life on an ongoing basis. If you're committing to a pledge to eat more fruit and vegetables, after a few weeks you may find that you have a roster of tried-and-tested recipes that are becoming easier to prepare with every attempt.

Admittedly, it's tiring to even think about implementing some of the changes we've outlined, so cut yourself some slack and recognize the sterling work you've already done in trying to make a difference to your life. If implementing a whole suite of changes right across your life is too daunting, scale it down a little. For the first week, focus on one or two changes to your routine in each area of your life. Give them a month to bed in properly, and then adopt another one or two new habits. Within a month, you should begin to see changes. After three months, you should start to see real progress.

If, after three months, little has improved, or things have got worse, review what's going wrong. Do you need to refine the route to your goals? Do you need to take another look at the steps required to reach them? What have you learnt from the last three months that will help you reformulate your plan?

Once you start seeing for yourself the benefits of establishing what is really important in your life, and eliminating everything else, you'll see the world through new eyes. Your passions, your relationships, your goals will all assume the status they deserve in your life, instead of jostling for your attention. With your mind now freed from the thankless cycle of buying into consumer culture and checking the Instagram stories from vacuous celebrities, you may even find new interests and new outlets for your talents.

Although minimalism is ostensibly about taking things away from our cluttered lives, it's really about adding richness and color and meaning. It's about identifying the aspects of our lives that we truly love and which nourish us. It's about trusting ourselves and leading the life we've always wanted.

So if you haven't done it yet, start clearing the place out. Roll up your sleeves and attack that attic. Straighten up that sideboard. Whip into shape that wardrobe. And remember: you can't reach for tomorrow's opportunities if your hands are full of yesterday's junk!

REFERENCES

1. Sanburn, J. (2015), 'America's Clutter Problem': https://time.com/3741849/americas-clutter-problem [Accessed 30 October 2019]

2. Rodgers, L. (2015), 'Where Do Your Old Clothes Go?': www.bbc.co.uk/news/magazine-30227025 [Accessed 30 October 2019]

3. Candy, L. (2019), 'Stella McCartney Pens an Open Letter to the Fashion Industry': www.thetimes.co.uk/magazine/style/stella-mccartney-pens-an-urgent-letter-to-the-fashion-industry-8hnnfdhjw [Accessed 30 October 2019]

4. Jardim, E. (2017), 'What 10 Years of Smartphone Use Means for the Planet': www.greenpeace.org/international/story/6913/what-10-years-of-smartphone-use-means-for-the-planet [Accessed 30 October 2019]

5. Schor, J. and Thompson, C. J. (2014), *Sustainable Lifestyles and the Quest for Plenitude*. London: Yale University Press.

6. McKeown, G. (2014), *Essentialism: The Disciplined Pursuit of Less*. London: Virgin Books.

7. Oliver, M. (1990), 'The Summer Day,' *House of Light*, Boston: Beacon Press.

8.   James, W. (1890), *The Principles of Psychology.* New York: Dover Publications, p.291.

9.   Belk, R. W. (1988), 'Possessions and the Extended Self,' *Journal of Consumer Research*, 15(2): 139–168.

10. Ibid., p.159.

11. Ibid., p146.

12. Roster, C. A., et al. (2016), 'The Dark Side of Home: Assessing Possession "Clutter" on Subjective Well-being,' *Journal of Environmental Psychology*, 46: 32–41.

13. Sanburn, J. (2015), 'America's Clutter Problem': https://time.com/3741849/americas-clutter-problem [Accessed 30 October 2019]

14. Vartanian, L., et al. (2017), 'Clutter, Chaos and Overconsumption: The Role of Mind-Set in Stressful and Chaotic Food Environments,' *Environment and Behavior,* 49(2): 215–23

15. Cutting, J. E., and Armstrong, K. L. (2016), 'Facial Expression, Size, and Clutter: Inferences From Movie Structure to Emotion Judgments and Back,' *Attention, Perception, & Psychophysics,* 78(3): 891–901.

16. Sanburn, J. (2015), 'America's Clutter Problem': https://time.com/3741849/americas-clutter-problem [Accessed 30 October 2019]

17. MacVean, M. (2014), 'For Many People, Gathering Possessions is Just the Stuff of Life,' *Los Angeles Times*, 21 March.

18. 'Self Storage UK FAQs,' Self Storage Association United Kingdom: www.ssauk.com/about-us/self-storage-uk-faqs [Accessed 1 November 2019]

19. 'Money Income in 1972 of Families and Persons in the United States (Advance Data from March 1973 Current Population Survey),' US Department of Commerce: www2.census.gov/prod2/popscan/p60-087.pdf [Accessed 1 December 2019]

20. Rubin, G. (2019), *Outer Order, Inner Calm: Declutter and Organize to Make More Room for Happiness*. London: Hodder & Stoughton.

21. Jacobs, T. (2019), 'Having a Sense of Purpose Helps You Live Longer,' *Pacific Standard Magazine*, 24 May.

22. Wrzesniewski, A. and Dutton, J. E. (2001), 'Crafting a Job: Revisioning Employees as Active Crafters of Their Work,' *Academy of Management Review*, 26(2): 179–201.

23. Schwantes, M. (2018), 'Warren Buffett Says Your Greatest Measure of Success at the End of Your Life Comes Down to 1 Word': www.inc.com/marcel-schwantes/warren-buffett-says-it-doesnt-matter-how-rich-you-are-without-this-1-thing-your-life-is-a-disaster.html [Accessed 6 November 2019]

24. Rhimes, S. (2015), *Year of Yes*. New York: Simon & Schuster.

25. Morrison, T. (1977) *Song of Solomon*. London: Vintage Books, p.179.

26. *EU Business News* (2019), 'UK shoppers own £10 billion worth of clothing they don't wear': https://www.business-news.eu/2019-uk-shoppers-own-10-billion-worth-of-clothing-they-don-t-wear [Accessed 6 November 2019]

27. Greenpeace International (2016), 'Black Friday: Greenpeace calls timeout for fast fashion': www.greenpeace.org/international/press-release/7566/black-friday-greenpeace-calls-timeout-for-fast-fashion [Accessed 6 November 2019]

28. Laville, S. (2018), 'Tyres and Synthetic Clothes "Big Cause of Microplastic Pollution",' *The Guardian*, 22 November.

29. Greenpeace International (2016), 'Black Friday: Greenpeace calls timeout for fast fashion': www.greenpeace.org/international/press-release/7566/black-friday-greenpeace-calls-timeout-for-fast-fashion [Accessed 6 November 2019]

30. Candy, L. (2019), 'Stella McCartney Pens an Open Letter to the Fashion Industry': www.thetimes.co.uk/magazine/style/stella-mccartney-pens-an-urgent-letter-to-the-fashion-industry-8hnnfdhjw [Accessed 30 October 2019]

31. Sample, L. (2010) 'The Price of Happiness? £50,000pa,' *The Guardian*, 6 September.

32. Brickman, P., et al. (1978), 'Lottery Winners and Accident Victims: Is Happiness Relative?,' *Journal of Personality and Social Psychology*, 36(8): 917–27.

33. Ramsey, D. (2003), *The Total Money Makeover: A Proven Plan for Financial Fitness* (2013 Edition). Nashville: Thomas Nelson, p.51.

34. Monbiot, G. (2013), 'Materialism: A System That Eats Us from the Inside Out': *The Guardian*, 9 December.

35. American Psychological Association (2014), 'What Psychology Says About Materialism and the Holidays: Six Questions for Materialism Expert Tim Kasser, PhD,' 16 December: www.apa.org/news/press/releases/2014/12/materialism-holidays [Accessed 6 December 2019]

36. Schor, J. and Thompson, C. J. (2014), *Sustainable Lifestyles and the Quest for Plenitude*. London: Yale University Press.

37. Belton, P. (2016) 'How a Traumatised Dog Inspired a Sharing Economy Business': www.bbc.com/news/business-37894951 [Accessed 7 November 2019]

38. Ibid.

39. Harford, T. (2017), 'How Department Stores Changed the Way We Shop': www.bbc.com/news/business-40448607 [Accessed 29 November 2019]

40. Martin, E. (2019), 'The Government Shutdown Spotlights a Bigger Issue: 78% of US workers live paycheck to paycheck': www.cnbc.com/2019/01/09/shutdown-highlights-that-4-in-5-us-workers-live-paycheck-to-paycheck.html [Accessed 7 November 2019]

41. Sandstrom, G. W. and Dunn, E. W. (2014), 'Social Interactions and Well-Being: The Surprising Power of Weak Ties,' *Personality and Social Psychology Bulletin*, July 1, 40(6): p.910–22.

42. Chowdhry, A. (2016), 'Most of Your Facebook Friends Are Not Your Real Friends, Says Study,' 30 January: www.forbes.com/sites/amitchowdhry/2016/01/30/most-facebook-friends-are-not-your-real-friends-says-study #3b278485757d [Accessed 1 December 2019]

43. Konnikova, M. (2013), 'How Facebook Makes Us Unhappy,' *New Yorker*, 10 September.

44. Burke, M., et al. (2010), 'Social Network Activity and Social Well-Being,' *Proceedings of the SIGCHI Conference on Human Factors in Computing Systems, Atlanta, Georgia*, April 10–15.

45. Konnikova, M. (2013), 'How Facebook Makes Us Unhappy,' *New Yorker*, 10 September.

46. Hartung, R. (2018), 'Massive Study Confirms That Loneliness Increases Risk of Dementia,' *Medical Express*, 29 October.

47. Vogel, E, et al. (2014), 'Social Comparison, Social Media, and Self-Esteem,' *Psychology of Popular Culture*, 3(4): 206–222.

48. Hunt, M. et al. (2018), 'No More FOMO: Limiting Social Media Decreases Loneliness and Depression,' *Journal of Social & Clinical Psychology*, 37(10).

49. Hydzik, A. (2016), 'Using Lots of Social Media Accounts Linked to Anxiety': www.futurity.org/social-media-depression-anxiety-1320622-2 [Accessed 18 September, 2019]

50. Winnick, M. (2016), 'Putting a Finger on our Phone Obsession: Mobile Touches': https://blog.dscout.com/mobile-touches [Accessed September 21, 2019]

51. Chamberlain, L. (2017), 'US Mobile Useage in 2017: Stats You Need to Know': https://geomarketing.com/us-mobile-usage-in-2017-stats-you-need-to-know [Accessed 23 September, 2019]

52. Solon, O. (2017), 'Ex-Facebook President Sean Parker: Site Made to Exploit Human "Vulnerability",' *The Guardian*, November 9

53. Ibid.

54. Adams, T. (2015), 'Sherry Turkle: I Am Not Anti-Technology, I Am Pro-Conservationist,' *The Guardian*, 18 October.

55. Lally, P., et al. (2010), 'How Habits Are Formed: Modelling Habit Formation in the Real World,' *European Journal of Social Psychology*, 40: 998–1009.

56. Buettner, D., Skemp, S. (2016), 'Blue Zones: Lessons from the World's Longest Lived,' *American Journal of Lifestyle Medicine*, 10(5): 318–21

57. Rosero-Bixby, L., et al. (2013), *Vienna Yearbook of Population Research*, 11: 109–136.

58. World Health Organization, 'Physical Activity and Adults': www.who.int/dietphysicalactivity/factsheet_adults/en [Accessed 30 November, 2019]

59. Clear, J. (2018), *Atomic Habits*. London: Random House Business Books, p.31.

60. Lally, P., et al. (2010), 'How Habits Are Formed: Modelling Habit Formation in the Real World,' *European Journal of Social Psychology*, 40: 998–1009.

61. Royal College of Psychiatrists (2017), 'Debt and Mental Health': www.rcpsych.ac.uk/mental-health/problems-disorders/debt-and-mental-health [Accessed 27 September, 2019]

62. American Psychological Association (2014), 'What Psychology Says About Materialism and the Holidays: Six Questions for Materialism Expert Tim Kasser, PhD,' 16 December: www.apa.org/news/press/releases/2014/12/materialism-holidays [Accessed 6 December 2019]

63. Murthy, V. (2017), 'Work and the Loneliness Epidemic (Harvard Business Review': www.vivekmurthy.com/single-post/2017/10/10/Work-and-the-Loneliness-Epidemic-Harvard-Business-Review [Accessed 11 October, 2019]

64. Cigna.com (2018), 'New Cigna Study Reveals Loneliness at Epidemic Levels in America': www.cigna.com/newsroom/news-releases/2018/new-cigna-study-reveals-loneliness-at-epidemic-levels-in-america [Accessed 10 October, 2019]

65. Whitman, W. (1855), 'I Sing the Body Electric,' *The Complete Walt Whitman: Drum-Taps, Leaves of Grass, Patriotic Poems, Complete Prose Works, The Wound Dresser, Letters* (2017 Edition), CDED, p182.

66. Lally, P., et al. (2010), 'How Habits Are Formed: Modelling Habit Formation in the Real World,' *European Journal of Social Psychology*, 40: 998–1009.

HAY HOUSE TITLES OF RELATED INTEREST

YOU CAN HEAL YOUR LIFE, the movie,
starring Louise Hay & Friends
(available as a 1-DVD program, an expanded
2-DVD set, and an online streaming video)
Learn more at www.hayhouse.com/louise-movie

THE SHIFT, the movie,
starring Dr Wayne W. Dyer
(available as a 1-DVD program, an expanded
2-DVD set, and an online streaming video)
Learn more at www.hayhouse.com/the-shift-movie

WHAT YOUR CLUTTER IS TRYING TO TELL YOU:
Uncover the Message in the Mess and Reclaim Your Life
by Kerri L. Richardson

THE YEAR OF LESS:
How I Stopped Shopping, Gave Away My Belongings
and Discovered Life Is Worth More Than Anything
You Can Buy in a Store
by Cait Flanders

THE ART OF EXTREME SELF-CARE:
Transform Your Life One Month at a Time
by Cheryl Richardson

The above titles are available at hayhouse.co.uk and hayhouse.com

Hay House Podcasts
Bring Fresh, Free Inspiration Each Week!

Hay House proudly offers a selection of life-changing audio content via our most popular podcasts!

Hay House Meditations Podcast

Features your favorite Hay House authors guiding you through meditations designed to help you relax and rejuvenate. Take their words into your soul and cruise through the week!

Dr. Wayne W. Dyer Podcast

Discover the timeless wisdom of Dr. Wayne W. Dyer, world-renowned spiritual teacher and affectionately known as "the father of motivation." Each week brings some of the best selections from the 10-year span of Dr. Dyer's talk show on Hay House Radio.

Hay House Podcast

Enjoy a selection of insightful and inspiring lectures from Hay House Live events, listen to some of the best moments from previous Hay House Radio episodes, and tune in for exclusive interviews and behind-the-scenes audio segments featuring leading experts in the fields of alternative health, self-development, intuitive medicine, success, and more! Get motivated to live your best life possible by subscribing to the free Hay House Podcast.

Find Hay House podcasts on iTunes, or visit www.HayHouse.com/podcasts for more info.

HAY HOUSE

Look within

Join the conversation about latest products,
events, exclusive offers and more.

f Hay House UK

🐦 @HayHouseUK

📷 @hayhouseuk

❤️ healyourlife.com

We'd love to hear from you!